Priceless Dream:

The Story of the Dallas Cowboys #1 Fan

Carolyn M. Price

with

Anwar Jamison

ISBN: 0-692-84252-7
ISBN-13: 978-0-692-84252-2

DEDICATION

I dedicate this book to God, my family, my Cowboys family and all of my friends who are too plentiful to name individually, but all special to me individually. I love you all.

CONTENTS

ACKNOWLEDGMENTS

I would like to thank my pastor, Porter Perry, his wife Marla, and the entire Temple of Prayer family. I would also like to thank my supervisor, Alfred Akinola and his wife Victoria, the entire staff of Naiman Community Health Services, the great city of Dallas, Booker T. Washington Technical High School, Royce West, David Wells, and the entire Dallas Cowboys organization.

I would like to give a special thanks to Mr. Jerry Jones, his wife Gene, his children Stephen (Karen), Charlotte (Shy) and Jerry Jr. and all of his grandchildren whom I've watched grow up. I would also like to thank every single player who has ever suited up for the Dallas Cowboys, our original coach Tom Landry, and all of our other coaches who guided our young men on their journey and were so kind to me: Jimmy Johnson, Barry Switzer, Chan Gailey, Dave Campo, Bill Parcells, Wade Phillips and Jason Garrett.

FOREWORD

I'm Eugene "The Hit Machine" Lockhart, All-Pro linebacker for the Dallas Cowboys. I joined the Cowboys in 1984. The highlight of my career was setting the NFL record for most tackles in a season with 222. Ms. Price is always present amongst the many Cowboys fans waving and cheering for the players before and after the games. A lot of fans wait around to meet the players, get autographs and take pictures, but of all the fans you see, Ms. Price is the one who stands out. She always has her Dallas Cowboys gear on from head to toe. She is always dressed for the occasion and impossible to miss.

She has the type of personality that screams, "You're going to love me, and you're going to know that I'm the Dallas Cowboys #1 fan! I'm going to be here every time you come out of that tunnel, so just get used to seeing me." When you see someone that has that kind of attitude, you can't help but to be drawn to them. The first time I saw her was the very first time I came running out of the tunnel as a rookie for a preseason game against the Pittsburgh Steelers. From then on, it just became everywhere I went:

every Cowboys function, every autograph session, every tailgate, and every single thing that involves the Dallas Cowboys, if nobody else is going to be there, you're going to see Ms. Price.

Not only is she going to be there, but you're going to hear that voice above every other voice yelling, "How about them Cowboys!"

After seeing her at all these different events, one time she said, "If there's anything I can do for you as a person, off the field, you can call me." We exchanged phone numbers, and that was when our relationship transitioned into a friendship, as opposed to just a player and fan relationship. When you see someone who's that loving, dedicated and kind, you want to be friends with them. You want that type of relationship with them.

There have been times when I needed to talk to someone about an issue, and I couldn't get in touch with The Cowboys, and she would be the one to make some things happen for me. Not that I couldn't call Tom Landry or Jimmy Johnson back when we played, but she had some different people that she could call that could do different things, and those were people that I didn't have relationships with.

For her to have been a Dallas Cowboys fan since the 60's, that's total dedication. She's been a Dallas Cowboys fan longer than some of us have been alive. She has touched each and every one of our hearts in all different types of ways. Even during our 1-15 season, when we were at our absolute low point, she was always energetic and just as dedicated. She would always let the other fans, and so-called fans, who might have dropped their heads know: real

Cowboys fans, real Cowboys players, real Cowboys teams, all stick together through thick and thin whether we win, lose or draw, we bleed silver and blue. That's the type of person she is and has always been, and I'm sure she's raised her kids, grandkids, and everyone around her to be Cowboys fans for life.

She's just an awesome person, and I'm so glad that I've gotten a chance to know her, not only as a fan, but also as a friend. She's an even better friend than she is a fan. She's a better mother and grandmother than she is a fan. She always finds time to get it all in, be the best at everything she does and surround herself with good people. We thank her for all of her dedication, well wishes and thoughts.

She knows every single person in the Cowboys organization, and when they don't get something done, she lets Jerry and Stephen Jones know about it. Since we've been friends, we have done personal appearances together. She has come to a lot of my tailgate parties and other events that I've hosted with the Dallas Cowboys. Overall, I can really say that we have developed a very strong friendship. I love her, and I know she loves me. Ms. Price is just simply the best, and I wish her the best of luck with this book and in every other aspect of her life.

-Eugene "The Hit Machine" Lockhart #56

1 HOME SWEET HOME

When you approach Ms. Price's house, the Dallas Cowboys flag drifting back and forth will alert you to fact that the home belongs to a fan of the Cowboys. However, that's far from unusual. After all, this is Dallas, and seeing the team's blue star logo outside of homes is as common as seeing Christmas decorations in December anywhere in America.

Seeing Ms. Price herself, clad in Dallas Cowboys gear, with a shiny star earring in each ear, and finger nails, bracelets, watch, necklace, visor, shades, and any other imaginable accessory present, reveals the notion that she's cut from a different cloth than the average fan of a professional football team. But still, there are other fans who emerge from their homes attired in an array of accessories celebrating their team of choice on a weekly basis. This is America, and football is akin to a religion for millions of faithful fans throughout the country.

However, there's a room inside of her home that provides undeniable proof that Ms. Price holds a singular place in Cowboys' lore. The room is her own extraordinary shrine. It is affirmation of her dedicated fandom. Someone could spend every waking moment online scouring every inch of cyberspace, sparing no expense, and still not be able to replicate the contents of the room.

A cursory glance at the walls reveals pictures with virtually everyone who's anyone or has been anyone in the Dallas Cowboys organization since the beginning. The players are there, the coaches are there, front office executives, staff, and the owner: they're all there. Sitting on tables and in boxes are other pictures with countless other figures who've passed through and etched their name in the Cowboys' history. There are posters, flyers, old ticket stubs, game programs, programs from team events, and almost anything else imaginable. Seeing all of this let's a person know: this is another level. That's before you get to the closet.

In a closet in the rear of the room, there are jerseys. There are so many jerseys that you can't tell whether or not the door can actually close. There are more jerseys hanging in that closet than some people have shirts of any type hanging in theirs. A lot of people collect jerseys. You might wonder: what's so special about that? When you get up close enough to the jerseys to examine them, you see what's so special about them. They've all been autographed: every single one of them. It's a closet stuffed over capacity with nothing but jerseys signed by the men who wore those jerseys for the Dallas Cowboys. Naming each and every name on every jersey would be overkill. What's important to know is that they're all there: "Too Tall" Jones, Tony Dorsett, Roger Staubach, Drew Pearson, Troy Aikman, Michael Irvin, and Emmitt Smith and on and on and on. If you can name them, chances are, they are there. By this point, if you don't already know, you'd probably ask, "Who is this woman with pictures all over her home hugging every single significant figure in the history of the Dallas Cowboys?" That's Ms. Carolyn Price: the Dallas Cowboys' #1 Fan.

I was born on November 27, 1943 in Dallas, Texas. The Dallas Cowboys were born in 1960, but I'll get to that part of the story soon enough: first things first. In our family, there were a total of nine children, but one died as a baby so I never had a chance to know him. He was born and had passed away before I got here. His name was Jim. I believe he had pneumonia. Back in those days, you didn't always know exactly what someone died of: especially young children. Of course, the medical field is a lot more advanced than it was in the 1940's.

The first born was Clara Jean Hill, followed by Gary Floyd Hill, then me, Carolyn Mopping. After me, there was Sandra Mopping, then Willie Harold Mopping, Florence Mopping, Phyllis Mopping and Roger Lee Mopping. My big sister Clara Jean was a very, very stern person and served as our protector. She didn't like for anyone to bother us. If someone did, she would not hesitate to fight and defend us. She wasn't the type of person that people wanted to be the enemy of. She was very protective of me in particular, but they all got angry, at times, because my mother favored me.

As far as stature, Willie, who we called Buck, was the tallest of my brothers and sisters, then Roger, the baby boy. Buck might have reached right around six feet tall. My brother Gary Floyd was very nice and mild-mannered: he was the sweetheart. Back in those days, when we were younger, people would call him slow, because he didn't get the best grades in school. But he was one of those people who had a knack for catching on to things really quickly. He was the type of person that was living proof that there were different types of education. There are some people who are considered book smart, and others who are smart in other ways. His strengths didn't really show up in a grade school classroom, but he was excellent at picking things up in the real world.

Sandra was also just a very sweet person. She had a very kind nature, but she was no pushover. Some people thought that she was because she was so sweet, and they tried to pick on her. People found out the hard way when they did that. She didn't play, no matter how sweet of a personality she had.

When I was a young girl, we lived in North Dallas. Very early in my childhood, we moved to a set of housing projects in North Dallas called Roseland Homes. I was about five or six years old at the time of the move. We lived at 3503 Lafayette in Roseland Homes. We had lived on Munger Avenue originally. The projects looked somewhat like the expensive brick high-rise apartments that they are paying a lot of money for nowadays, but with only two stories. They were well-built, and the brick seemed to be of a higher quality than the brick today, as most things are.

There were some small one-bedroom apartments attached to the end of the building on most of the units, and usually single women lived in those. We had four bedrooms in our apartment: three upstairs and one downstairs. Mom and dad slept in the bedroom downstairs next to the kitchen and living room. There were no air-conditioning units in the apartments at the time. We used to have big fans, and we had to put ice in front of them to keep the homes cool in the summer. There was one stove in the middle of the living room to heat the entire house in the winter. Sometimes, we would have to use the oven in the kitchen as well to stay warm when the weather changed.

Even though they were called "the projects," we were raised to take care of the place where we lived. As a result, they were not just some ran-down buildings. We were all poor, but none of us thought of it that way. It was a different time and a different class of people as far as the values that they had.

With the number of people living in our house, we had to get used to sleeping close to others. Like most families in the projects, there were far more occupants in the household than the number of bedrooms. Families got creative with the way that they placed kids to sleep. It was not uncommon to have someone sleeping on a roll away bed in the kitchen. In our home, the boys had bunk beds in their bedroom. I never will forget, Floyd slept in one and Buck slept in the other. Then, there was another room that had twin beds, and that was Sandra, Florence and Phyllis' room. Clara Jean and I shared a room, and there were twin beds in there also. When Clara Jean left home, I was in there by myself and I refused to let anyone share with me. At least that's what they said I did anyway, ha!

Growing up, I had to learn how to cook because my mother was sick a lot, and she depended on me to take up the slack and help out during those times when she didn't feel well. She used to coach me through preparing a meal from start to finish. She was very detailed about what to do every step of the way. She worked in servant quarters so she knew how to do it all. I took pride in seeing if I could make things exactly the way that she made them.

I felt a tremendous sense of achievement if I made something so well that you couldn't tell whether or not she had made it. That was my goal. I remember when she first showed me how to fix bread from scratch. To this day, after all these years, I still use the recipe: meal, flour, salt, sugar, baking powder and an egg. She would say, "Beat it real good, Carolyn. Beat it real good."

"Go in that kitchen girl, you go in that kitchen and you get that stuff out I told you," she would tell me.

"Ok, Mama." I always made sure I obeyed Mama. I had to obey my mother. In my mind, as a child, it was just the right thing to do. I didn't understand my siblings or friends who were more rebellious. I just did what she said. It was just that simple to me back then.

Just as the children in most large families did, my siblings and I divided ourselves up into cliques. We didn't mean any harm by it, and we didn't love any of our siblings less than others, but it's just what kids tend to do. Florence and Sandra were really close, and they hung together a lot. Sandra and I were the same age, and I would end up taking up for Phyllis, while Sandra would take up for Florence. Clara Jean didn't get caught up in our little games as much because she was the oldest. She would just get on any of us when she felt like it.

Of the boys, I would take up for Buck and he became like my baby. Floyd got sick of me and Sandra because we were always doing something to him and he would try to fight us. It was never too serious, but just natural sibling rivalries that developed amongst brothers and sisters. Sometimes, there was pain involved though, ha!

One time, Floyd got tired of me for something I was probably doing to him, and he was jumping on me. He had gotten really mad and was going to beat me up, so Sandra went to the stove and heated up the curling irons that we used for our hair. She ran up to him and stuck them to his back and he screamed, "Ahhhhhhhhhhh! Someone shot me!"

She said, "Ain't nobody shot you fool, I burned you! You better get up off Carolyn!"

We were always into something. Pretty much

12

any form of mischief you could imagine, we were into it. My oldest sister Clara Jean would get on us a lot. When mom was away, she was like the corrections officer keeping everyone in their place. She would make all of us sit down and obey, and didn't let us have any fun. You would think it would be easier being watched by our sister, but that wasn't the case. When Mama would come home, I would tell on her.

"Mama, Clara made us sit down and wouldn't let us get up. She wouldn't let us do anything," I would say. Clara would eyeball me with an icy glare that let me know I'd have to deal with her later for my act of defiance.

"You leave my babies alone," my mom would tell her. At that point, I'd probably be hiding behind Mama doing something like sticking my tongue out at Clara Jean, or some other act to taunt her. My mother had a special place in her heart for my baby brother Roger and me. She loved him, and he was really spoiled. Looking back, I don't think it was necessarily that we were her favorites, but she understood certain roles that were for us to play. She needed me to grow up and provide some help. For whatever reason, she felt that I was the one to do it. Now that I'm grown, I understand. I didn't understand back then. I used to feel like I was being singled out and I took it as a negative thing.

At times, I felt like my mother was picking on me. If I made a certain grade that was lower than what she expected and she got on me, I'd try to deflect the attention back to my brothers or sisters. I'd say "Mama they're not doing good either," and she'd say, "Well, you just do good! Don't worry about what they're doing." There was a different set of expectations for me. I can take it as a compliment now, but I didn't see it that way then.

I really enjoyed going to school when I was growing up, and I excelled at it. I always took my studies seriously, and I was always excited to learn new information. Learning new things was like playing a game to me: it was fun. It was like I was moving around an imaginary board game every time I learned something new. I was determined to be the best that I could possibly be in my studies. My brother Floyd was older than me, but I was really smart, so we ended up in class together when we were younger.

In one particular class, I used to let him copy off my work because it was really hard for him, even though I was the younger sibling. The teacher was Ms. Brown. To my surprise, Ms. Brown knew that I was letting him copy my work all along. Like the average little kid, I was silly enough to think that she couldn't tell what was going on. She told my mother and I thought I was going to really get it.

My mother said, "I'm not going to whup you, because I did tell you to help him, so I guess I can't be too mad at you." Being the protector of my brothers and sisters was a role that I would grow into more and more as time went on. That wasn't the type of help that she meant, but at least I got the benefit of the doubt for doing something about it. The way we were raised back then, if a teacher told on you, it pretty much meant a whuppin was coming.

Even though she wouldn't hesitate to get on us, my mom really was sweet. Being sweet didn't mean she was quiet though. My baby sister Phyllis and my dad were really quiet. She took after him. That's something you could never say about me. I took more after my mother. I was more outspoken and aggressive.

Our home was a two-story house. Nowadays, they would call it a townhouse. I had no idea that we lived in the ghetto until someone told me. That's usually the way it is for children. When the love is present, and you don't feel like you're missing out on anything, you're satisfied, and I was no different. At that early age, you don't really have a grasp of ghetto, low-income, working class, or any of those labels that get applied to you.

My parents were really good parents in the sense that they wanted what was best for us and did everything in their power to make it happen. My mother would get on us for a lot of different things. It was around this time that I first noticed that she seemed to be on me more than the others. I couldn't wrap my mind around the fact that she did that. One thing about parents though: they know each of their children, what they are capable of, and what they are not capable of. Even though I was not the oldest, I became the one who would always have a lot of responsibility placed on my shoulders. I had no way of knowing that I was being prepared for a lot of what would come later on in my life.

My mom would say, "Carolyn make sure you fix them something to eat," or "make sure you help them with their lesson," or "make sure you help Florence and Phyllis get their hair done for school tomorrow." So, that became a part of my routine. I got used to making sure that they were all taken care of, and then I would worry about myself.

I was always an active person when it came to interacting with my friends and peers. I was far from a wallflower. I was more of a social butterfly. I participated in quite a few activities, and when something was going on, I always wanted to be involved. I never wanted to feel like I was wasting time. I understood the value of time from a very early age, so wasting it was not an option. That's something that was always unacceptable to me, and that's a trait that I carried with me as I grew older and became an adult.

Two of my best friends from back then are still good friends of mine today: Judy Fleming and Fred Walker. In the second grade, Judy moved to Dallas from Austin. By the time we made it to the third grade, we became really good friends. She had a brother, and her mom moved their family to Dallas to establish a better life for them. I don't remember the exact moment I met her, but I know we hit it off pretty quickly and have been friends ever since. She said I took her lunch from her when I first met her though. I don't remember anything like that and I'd like to believe it's not true, ha! I can't guarantee it though. It was just one of those relationships that was meant to happen.

We attended J.W. Ray Elementary School that year. In those days, the elementary school only went up to the second grade. The next year, in third grade, we moved on to B.F. Darrell School, and we attended that school all the way through the 8th grade. Judy and Fred were in my homeroom, which was the primary class that you attended before you broke off and went to your other classes. Fred lived in Roseland where my family lived, so I would always see him, even outside of school. With Judy, it started out as one of those friendships where you only saw each other at school and made the most of the time you had. Over time, it developed into a great friendship outside of school as well.

Living in Roseland with us, Fred was close to my brothers and sisters as well. He saw everything we went through up close and personal. Most days, I would put on my bravest face and act like nothing was really going on, but often, I would be hurting inside, mostly if my parents were sick.

Living in the projects is usually associated with poverty, but back then, not everyone who lived in the projects were the poorest of the poor. There were people who lived around us who had pretty decent jobs at the time. There were people who worked for the post office, or Morton's, the big potato chip company. Some people then began to move to South Dallas, which had been all white up until that point. A lot of the school teachers and professionals were buying houses in South Dallas and Oak Cliff. We never got to experience that. We were basically just struggling to maintain as much as we could.

My mom, grandmother and a lot of others went across what people called "the track" to go to work. It wasn't literally across a track, but just further North, and that's where they worked. They worked in private homes, taking care of people's kids, washing, ironing and doing other domestic work, and then they would come back home. When it came to the other kids in the neighborhood, we really enjoyed each other. We stayed outdoors playing as much as we could, and we had a feeling of togetherness. That's one of the ironic things about how people deal with each other now compared to then. We might have had a lot of problems as a result of being poor, but one problem we didn't have was sticking together. In the summer, almost every yard would have a pallet in it, and we slept outdoors sometimes because it was so hot. For those who don't know, a pallet is just a makeshift bed from blankets or whatever you could put your hands on to make it comfortable enough.

We played a lot of different games and found plenty of ways to be entertained, but more than anything, skating was the preferred activity for all of us at that time. Everybody wanted one of two things for Christmas: a bicycle, or a pair of skates. We were really big-time skaters. We loved it.

We also had a swimming pool that we went to at Griggs Park. Griggs Park was named for Rev. Allen R. Griggs, who was one of the most important black men in the history of Dallas. He was born a slave in Georgia, but brought to Texas at the age of nine. In 1865, he experienced freedom for the first time at age 15. He became one of the most accomplished and well-known Baptist preachers of his time. He ended up establishing the first high school for black students in 1878, and that same year he established the first African-American newspaper in the state of Texas. Of course, we didn't think of any of this when we were kids, but our community was rich with a lot of history, and I'd like to think that we soaked up some of it even when we were not even aware of it.

This was early in the days of television when they were not nearly as common as they are now. Everybody didn't have a television set, but as with most everything else, where there was a will, there was a way. The mentality in our neighborhood was share and share alike. How do you share a TV you might wonder? Well, the ones who did have TV's would actually leave their windows open so people outside could stand in the yard and see the TV through the window. Can you imagine doing that now?

Occasionally, someone would lean out of a window and yell, "It's some colored folks on TV!" That was enough to start a stampede, ha! I don't care what was going on outside, everybody would stop what they were doing and get around a window to see somebody's TV. It was a really rare thing to see black people on TV back then. We needed something to identify with. So, when we got a chance to see a black person on TV, that was it for us, everything else stopped for a while.

It's impossible to explain what that did for our minds. People who see themselves represented in everything all the time can never imagine the emotion of seeing yourself represented when you rarely get the opportunity. The few black stars that we had back then became so important to us. We lived through them in a way. Those rare glimpses that we got of them served as a reminder that there was something else out there somewhere. We didn't know where that somewhere was, or how to get there, but sometimes you just needed to know that it was there.

The funniest part about it is, we even worked our creativity into our TV watching experience. Television sets were not color yet, they were still black and white. So, we would take some colored plastic wrap and stretch it over the screen to get some homemade color, ha! Red plastic, yellow plastic, blue plastic, green plastic: it didn't matter. You could put it on the screen and get you a little Technicolor.

Our creativity and resourcefulness had no limit. That went on until midnight, when television went off. Of course, programming wasn't available twenty-four hours a day back then. Besides television, we listened to a lot of our favorite programs on the radio. Radio was still really big back then for shows. We loved listening to the music of our favorite singers, of course, but back then, we still had actual shows on radio too.

2 COMING OF AGE

For Ms. Price, The weekend of a game does not merely consist of the day when the game is played. There are always a number of events put on by various groups in the days leading up to the game, and the Cowboys' extended family turns them into family reunions. On this particular day, Ms. Price is at a dinner at a local hotel, which features a few current players answering questions from local media in front of fans, in an elegant setting. Fans pay for a plate and an opportunity to spend a little intimate time with select players. While patrons are waiting for the event to begin, fans mingle with each other in an adjacent room. There are tables filled with jerseys of current and former players, along with various other memorabilia for sale. From time to time, former players stroll through. One approaches Ms. Price, who is standing by speaking with a couple of other fans.

"Hey, Ms. Price. How you doing?" He reaches out and hugs her.

"You used to play for the Cowboys," she recognizes him

as she returns the hug. "Number 35?"

"Number 25," he corrects her. "25," she repeats, "alright." He's not one of the famous former Cowboys' players and he blends in amongst the fans at the event. No one is approaching him and asking for an autograph, and not many people appear to know who he is. Ms. Price does.

"You got it. So how you been?"

"Ms. Price been fine."

"That's good. I know you're alright. I see you," he replies.

"I'm doing good baby. I ran out here to see my babies and now I think I might head over to the hotel where they're staying."

"Oh, where they at now?"

"At the Gaylord."

"Ok. I think I might roll over there. They could have put us somewhere like that. They at the Gaylord now, huh?" he laughs.

"Yeah, but where you were at was nice too," Ms. Price adds. "You know what? Let me tell you something. Detroit is going to curse the day that they put us on the schedule."

"They're going down?"

"Oh yeah, we gon' tear 'em up. I'ma sick my cheerleaders on 'em."

"To get 'em distracted?"

"Uh huh, I'ma say, hey girls, kick your legs up real high." She's briefly distracted as a woman stands on her side trying to get her attention.

"Hey darling! How are you doing honey?" Ms. Price embraces the woman and they began to talk about the events of

the weekend.

"You remember what I told you?"

"Oh yeah, everything's better. It's great," the woman replies.

"Sometimes you gotta go that route, darling," Ms. Price tells her.

"Thank you."

"King of kings, lord of lords, ha!" Without any additional confirmation, it's obvious that the woman is just one of many friends who've sought the advice of Ms. Price, and has returned to let her know that her advice was heeded and appreciated.

"Look how cute I am, check out this shape," Ms. Price tells her. "Am I a brickhouse or what?"

"You go, Ms. Price."

"Let me go and get my ring now." She goes back over to the player and speaks to him in hushed tones as she leans on his shoulder. He slides a ring off his finger and places it in Ms. Price's hand.

"I know you don't know what this is," she holds a ring in the air and playfully taunts her friend, "but this is a Super Bowl ring. The real deal darling."

"Now tell me how many players would take off their Super Bowl ring and give it to a fan?"

During this time, all of the residents of the projects were black, but there were white people who owned stores in the area around the projects. One family, the Raines family, owned a store in the projects and they used to bring their children with them to the store. They were decent people who always treated us with respect. This was a much different time period in Dallas, so to describe them as decent is saying a lot, and should be considered a compliment, because the majority of the white people we encountered did not treat us decently. This is when it was still not only acceptable, but expected, to treat black people as second-class citizens. In the Raines' store though, they treated us better than most. Sometimes when you grow up poor and you're a kid in a candy store, literally, sometimes the temptation could prove to be too much for some. It's not like we were walking around with a pocketful of money. This got a lot of kids in trouble for trying to steal.

Even if one of our brothers or friends may have stolen something out of the store, in The Raines' store, they would call our mom instead of getting the police involved, and allow her to discipline them. That alone was doing a big favor, because there's no telling how that police interaction might turn out. I don't know if it was just the fact that we were their customers and we were helping them make their living or what, but they didn't act like a lot of the others did towards us. I don't know where they lived or came from, but they were right there every day in the projects with us.

They had two stores: the one near our home and one in South Dallas. Mr. Raines wasn't as friendly as the ladies were: most white men were not. For some reason though, he would usually smile and be pleasant. They would always laugh and get a kick out of me because I was the one that would speak up and be more forward than the others. That was rare, because we had it ingrained deeply in us to say as little around white people as possible. It wasn't necessarily anything that needed to be explained. We just saw it, felt it, and picked up the habit.

They had a daughter named Sandra and a son named Robert, and they used to let them come by our home to play with us. They were both pretty close to me in age. They would be the only white children in the projects with all of us. Looking back, I wonder what that experience was like for them. I'm sure they looked back at that experience as they got older and realized how unusual it was, but as children, we didn't think much about it.

There was also a family, the Thompsons, whom my mother worked for. When they would travel and go out of town, Mama would bring their children home with us, or take one or two of us out to their house to stay there. It didn't seem odd to me then, but looking back, that said a lot about how well-respected my mother was to be trusted with their children, and at times, their home. We didn't really see a difference between us and them at that time because we were raised with these kids and Mama would discipline us all the same.

In the innocence of that age, I really didn't think of race that much. There was a series of events over time that revealed to me what race really meant to my life and the people around me. I learned from each of these events and interactions, and when I got older and had to go out and look for jobs and work for people, I experienced how mean people could really be. That was when I really understood racism. At this point, I had certain indications, but I had just accepted them as what life was.

One of the first lessons many of us learned about race was also the first time that most of us actually saw a dead person. He was a young guy from our neighborhood named Tommy Lee Walker. He was sentenced to death, and executed in the electric chair because they said he had raped a white woman. After the execution, they brought him back to the funeral home in the neighborhood, and many of us saw him there. This painted a really vivid picture that we never forgot. We had known people to die, and we had been to funerals, but not like this.

Everyone was talking about what happened, and it was a clear example that there were lines in life that we were not supposed to cross. There were black men back then who just looked at a white woman and were accused of raping them. A rape charge against a black man involving a white woman was an automatic death sentence for a black man in Texas at that time. There was a question among everybody in the community whether Tommy was guilty or not, and most folks didn't think he was, but it didn't matter.

There was a lot going on back then with

police brutality and the black people in the community. Many of those events would began to shape our awareness about race and what we were expected to do or not do.

One of our classmates, Mary Thomas, was the daughter of one of the first black police officers in Dallas. Another practice from back then that people would consider unimaginable nowadays was the fact that black police officers couldn't arrest white people. Imagine a black police officer witnessing a white person committing a crime, and being unable to do anything about it. That's unthinkable in the context of today's society. Actually, they couldn't really arrest black people either. When a black person needed to be arrested, they could only hold them and call the white police officers to let them come and arrest them. Imagine that! So, even if they were arresting someone black, the police had to call the police. That pretty much defeated the purpose of being the police.

We also noticed how there were always a lot of white people who came to the black community for a lot of different things, whether it was for music or dancing, or for barbecue or soul food. They could come into our neighborhoods freely, but we could not go into theirs. If we did go to their establishments, we had to go to the back door. They were always welcome around us.

I remember when we got a little older, Fred and other neighborhood boys talked about looking forward to the white girls who would sneak into the neighborhood to catch a black man, and how careful they had to be about it. If they were caught, they knew that chances were, they would be accused of rape. I guess the memory of what happened to Tommy wasn't enough to scare them from being tempted.

Going to the movies was another experience that was big in our lives. It was like therapy to go and sit in that dark room for a couple of hours and get lost in an entirely different world. It wasn't just the opportunity to see a story being told, it was a huge event for us. At the Majestic Theater downtown, we had to sit up in the balcony. Nowadays, the balcony is the place to be, but back then, it was the only place we could be. Sometimes, we used to throw papers and popcorn down on the people below because they wouldn't allow us down there.

We also couldn't go into a lot of the stores. Neiman Marcus, which was the main department store in the city, would not let a black person in unless they were a maid and they were with the person that they worked for. There was a family that lived near us that had five children. One of their daughters, Constance, was really, really light-skinned: so much so that a lot of people thought she was white.

We brought Constance along when we went to certain stores because we knew we could fool them, and she was the only one who would be allowed inside. She would go inside and get everything we wanted, and then afterwards we would tell them she was black and they would chase us, ha! For that split second though, we felt like we had got over. In our minds, it was a small way of striking a blow for the cause.

For the most part, buying the things we wanted out of the store just wasn't that realistic. Who had money for that? We didn't. Basically, any toy that was sold in the store, we would just make our own version of it, and be happy with that. We couldn't afford dolls, so if we wanted a doll, we made it. We'd get a soda water bottle, use some rope with a clothespin for the hair, put a dress on it and we had a doll.

Our minds were so creative that we would find a way to come up with a satisfactory version of whatever we wanted to play with. If we saw kites flying around, and decided that we wanted a kite, we'd take some newspaper, get some starch for glue and make our own kite. Other than that, we played the regular games that kids would play for entertainment: hide and go seek, kick the can, spin the bottle, little Sally Walker and others.

More than anything, there was a real sense of community where we lived. We had a lot of love for each other despite the fact that we were poor: or maybe it was because we were poor. In order to make it, we stuck together. It was a common thing to go to your neighbor's house and borrow a cup of sugar, or borrow a cup of shortening, some washing powder or a stick of butter. If you borrowed it, when that next month rolled around, you'd give it back. All of these things that we take for granted now, and have a lot of, were valuable commodities back then. We all helped each other when we could in order to make it through. I believe that our friendships lasted so long because they were built on such a solid foundation. We had so much in common because of our experiences. It made the bonds so much stronger between us.

However, no matter how much love was around, kids still loved to tease each other. One thing we were teased about was our last name: Mopping. That last name made us an easy target for obvious reasons. You could come up with all kinds of silly insults using the words mop, or mopping. They could be cruel.

When you were as poor as we were, hygiene could be a problem, especially for boys. For some reason, young boys generally just do not like to keep themselves clean. Taking baths never seems to be high up on their to-do list at a young age. I think that comes later when they start liking girls and caring what the girls think about them. I was never going to be teased about that, I made sure of it, but my brothers were sometimes. I was always clean and well-kept. I guess I wanted to make sure that I gave people as little ammunition as possible to make fun of me.

Wherever there are people with little money,

and a lot of time on their hands, you'll find people getting into things that they have no business dealing with. The Bible says that idle hands are the devil's workshop, and there are a lot of idle hands when you spend most of your time confined to one area. As creative as we were with our activities, there's only so many things you can do with little resources. This is not a new thing, and it certainly was a problem when we were young. Unfortunately, when I got a little older, I saw some of those idle hands turning to something that would become a recurring problem for many people around me: drugs.

Even though drugs are not a problem that is exclusive to poor people, it seems like they serve a different purpose for people in the ghetto. Self-medication is a real thing. A lot of times, people are trying to escape from their reality and turn to drugs as a way to do it. I thank God that I never personally had that struggle. I just never tried anything like that and I never had the urge to, but it affected a lot of people around me and would become a problem that would affect me in a second hand way for my entire life. Whether it was childhood friends, family members, adult friends, or Dallas Cowboys players, I saw the effects over and over of how drugs crippled people's lives and the lives of the people they love.

In the projects, there were kids my age sticking needles in their arms as early as twelve years old. They must have been practicing things that they had seen grown people do, because they were taking drugs that weren't really drugs and turning them into drugs. Sadly, they had the same mentality that we had with the toys. Just like when we couldn't afford real toys, we made them, well some of these kids used other substances as drugs because they couldn't get real drugs. They were shooting a substance into their arms called paragon. It was a medicine you could take for stomach discomfort.

Another substance they were using was called valo. Valo came from a tube that they would melt down from the inside of an inhaler: the kind you used to help clear your nose when it was stopped up. They would melt it down and it would turn really green. They would actually put this into a needle and shoot it into their arms the same way people shot heroin into their veins. It doesn't take much imagination to guess what happened to most of the boys who were doing that. Eventually, most of them graduated and began actually shooting heroin.

Sadly, this just became a normal part of life, especially growing up in the ghetto. In that environment, a lot of people picked up habits that they carried with them. You had to make it to the point where you could distinguish between what was right and what was wrong as soon as possible, because that line could become blurry in a hurry.

Growing up, there was a lot of domestic violence around us also. Well, nowadays we call it domestic violence, but back then it didn't seem so out of the ordinary because it was around us so much.

I'm thankful that I didn't have to see it in my household growing up, but I would find out later through personal experience, no one is exempt from it.

I remember Fred told me later on that he had to really re-program himself later in life, from being exposed to it so much at an early age. As a young boy, he had seen it so often that he thought it was what he was supposed to do when he got older. He had seen men fighting women so much growing up, that not only did he think it was acceptable, but he thought it was a sign of being masculine. He thought that it was simply how a man interacted with his woman. It is terrible to have your mind warped in that way by what you see at a young, impressionable age.

On the other side, there were a lot of girls who thought it was ok and settled for that because they had seen it so often. When things like this, along with drugs, drinking, and stealing become seen as normal, and not out of the ordinary, unhealthy situations can spring up all around you like weeds, and grow to choke you out later on when you least expect it.

In the projects, there were different little cliques and ways that kids managed to divide themselves up. Just like most people, you tend to stand next to people who you identify with, and we were no different. One of those ways was by the church that you attended. There were several churches in the neighborhood, and certain families attended certain churches. As a result, many of us became friends with kids from our church, and formed our immediate circles based on the church you attended. As a child, I attended Page's Temple Church of Christ on Thomas Avenue. I went to New Zion Baptist Church when we were really small kids, but when we moved to Roseland, we went to Page's Temple. We were there every Sunday without question. It wasn't an option, it was mandatory.

We would look like some little dolls with our high-top patent leather shoes on that my dad would shine up for us. We didn't have a lot of shoes so we had to make sure we kept our Sunday shoes together. We had really long, thick hair and it would be combed in a really pretty style. Daddy didn't come to church with us a lot. It was Mama who always attended church and made sure that we were right there with her. Daddy would help us get ready. He would put us in the bathtub two at a time, and then, help us get dressed. My younger siblings: Buck, Phyllis and Florence were my responsibility and I had to make sure that their clothes were neat and ready to go. That was just a part of the responsibility that my mom placed on me.

Page's Temple was a large church, one of the largest in the city at that time. When you entered, there were two sides to the church with the choir stand up the middle, behind the pulpit. We would go down front and praise God as we were taught to do, and I remember that the area around the altar felt like a special place. Those days were really building my foundation as a Christian and giving me so much energy that I would need to lean on in my life. I had no way of realizing it, but I was being spiritually trained to take on all of the adversity that was to come my way, similar to the way that a football player physically trains to take all the hits that they take out on the football field. God was training me to take all the hits that I would have to endure in life.

Our pastor, R. M. Jackson, was a great man of God. His presence wasn't that imposing physically. He was an average-sized man, or slightly above average, close to six feet tall maybe, but his presence was much bigger. He wasn't overly boisterous or loud, he was pretty soft-spoken, but his knowledge of the Bible and his passion for what he believed was larger than life. He was always emphasizing what was right and what was wrong. He talked it and he walked it. It wasn't only when he was in the pulpit delivering a sermon, but in our lives as a whole. He was such a devout Christian, as was his wife and his whole family. It set an example for me that became an important influence in my life.

We would walk back and forth to church, and every Sunday we had two services: a morning and an evening service. We would have Sunday School in the morning, followed by the early service and we would leave and go home. The evening service would begin around six or seven o'clock. By the time we got out of the night service, it would be about 10 or 11 o'clock pm. In order to get home, we had to walk right through the main drag at Thomas and Hall streets. For the black neighborhoods, that was one of the main intersections in town. It was that part of town where everyone could meet up and indulge in whatever their particular vice was. Everything illegal and illicit that people picture about those neighborhoods could be found in that area.

Our church was on Thomas, so we had to walk past the nightclubs to get home, and the streets were always full of people. It's ironic that everything we were being preached to about, and told to stay away from, were the things that we walked passed on our way to and from church. One thing that stands out in my mind to this day is how much the people out there respected us. The street people, the people who were called thugs, the people we were supposed to be worried about, would step aside and clear a way for us to walk through.

"These the church people," somebody would say as we'd pass. "Watch out. Let them come through." We walked right through all of the rhythm and blues, the dancing, the gambling and the drinking. When we walked through, all of that would cease, as we passed by. It was an early example for me that people can't simply be reduced to good or bad. It taught me not to judge people based on what other people say they are. People make decisions in life, but those decisions are not necessarily who those people are, it's what they decided to do. That was a valuable lesson for me to learn, because if I turned my back on everyone who had a problem with substance abuse, or gambling, I would've lost a lot of people, many who were able to straighten up and get back on track.

Later on, our church actually burned down. There were rumors that some outside people wanted the church, but the church wouldn't sell to them, so they burned it down. Another rumor was that people in the church burned it down for insurance money. As with anything, there are always rumors and there was no way for us to know. The church is still in existence in the Oak Cliff area, but in a different building. Our pastor's son is the pastor of the church now, Rev. Jackson. It is now known as First Pentecostal Church of God in Christ, and it was the first COGIC church in Dallas, so that's another piece of history that we were a part of.

We all attended the same school, but Judy didn't live in the projects with us. Her family was more well-off than ours, and they lived in their own house. Judy's family attended Pilgrim Rest Baptist Church, and I would visit their church on some Sundays. On other Sundays, she would come and visit our church. Her mother, Oggie, owned her own beauty shop that was simply called Oggie's Beauty Shop.

The shop was located at the corner of Thomas and Boll. Oggie was a great beautician and all of the black celebrities: actors, actresses, singers, and all were her clients. When they would come to Dallas to perform, Oggie was who they went to see to get their hair done. I'm talking about Ray Charles, Tina Turner, Chubby Checker, Sam Cooke, The Staples Singers and many more. You can name any black star from that time, and I'll bet you that they probably sat in Oggie's chair at some point and got their hair done.

Not only did she really have a special talent for doing hair, but she was also a really spirit-filled person. She could fix your hair, and she could help you fix your life at the same time because she would introduce you to Jesus. The word got around, and people began to seek her out more and more to become their beautician. Also, Pilgrim Rest was the church where many people worshipped when they came to Dallas. So, not only did the word spread around Dallas, but it also spread to the various celebrities by word of mouth when they were in town.

She was so much in demand that a lot of them even ended up going over to her house to get their hair done. Church was always her priority and she let everyone know that she stuck by her hours at the beauty shop, no matter what. She always made sure that she was home at a decent hour so she could be ready for Sunday School. Therefore, many of them had to get their hair done at her house.

Judy mentioned how Margie, one of Ray Charles' backup singers in the Raelettes, used to always ask Oggie to pray for Ray. Every time she would come she would say, "Pray for Ray, please make sure you pray for Ray." Of course as kids, we didn't know why. People were always praying for somebody around us. Looking back, I'm sure it was because of the heroin addiction that he suffered from. A great thing about Judy was that she didn't try to keep all of the star sightings to herself, which is what a lot of people would have done. Sometimes, she would call us and tip us off to let us know that a certain celebrity was over her house getting their hair done. One day, the phone rang and it was Judy.

"Guess who's over here! Chuck Berry!" she said. "Hurry up and get over here, but when you come, act like you're just passing by, like you're just in the neighborhood and happened to stop by."

"Chuck Berry! Ok, I'm coming right over," I told her.

"Don't come in here screaming, hollering and acting out. Just knock on the door calmly and act like you're visiting."

A few of us ended up in the house on the couch acting like we were reading magazines while we stared over the top of them at Chuck. I noticed Judy out of the corner of my eye twisting her face up, giving us the eye, and making gestures towards us with her head. I knew we were being quiet and I thought we were acting normal, so I couldn't figure out what was wrong. I just tried to be even quieter, and sit even more still. She told us later that a couple of us had the magazines turned upside down while we were pretending to read, ha! I guess we didn't do too good of a job acting normal.

Because her mom owned such a successful business, Judy was always several notches above us when it came to economic class, but the good thing about it was, it never made a difference in our relationship. She never acted as if she was better than us because we lived in the projects and she didn't. Our bond was strong and we had real love for one another. When she got older, her mother passed the beauty shop down to Judy. Judy still owns the beauty shop to this day. She works at the church and she does hair.

At that time, Sandra and I were a little more light-skinned than some of the other kids, and my dad would whup us if we would call the others black, or some of the other ugly things that kids used to say to each other. He would mostly hit me on the back of my hand. He never had to do much. Men usually don't have to because of their voices. It's funny, I guess I thought the same thing would work on my mom, because one time I threatened my mom, and thought my dad could save me.

"I'm going to tell Dad on you!" I told her. I don't know what in the world I was thinking, but I learned a quick lesson about that one. I never made that mistake again. She whupped me really good over that one, and Daddy didn't lift a finger or say a word to save me, ha!

My mother was the disciplinarian most of the

time when it was necessary. Dad probably whupped us two or three times total. I was smart enough to avoid getting whupped most of the time. I had pretty much figured out a system to stay out of the way. The smaller kids were always getting them. Clara Jean was also always getting them because she was always talking smart. With me, it was mostly when I would do something to an adult and they would find out about it: that's when I would get it. My brother might get into it with someone, and if someone said something to him, I was quick to take up for him.

"You're not going to talk to my brother like that," I'd say. But I still had no business talking to an adult like that. That was the cause of a lot of the discipline that came my way.

I remember the last whuppin my father gave me was for calling my sister out of her name. She was darker than I was, and as sad as it is to admit, growing up as black children, we saw that as something to tease someone about. It's no secret in the black community. We're all well aware of it and we learn that terrible behavior at an early age. You always had that as a weapon that you could pull out and hurt someone's feelings with if you had to. I don't remember what it was, but she had done something that made me really mad, and I called her a black panther. My dad got on me. I did that because we had a black panther lamp, and I suppose somehow in my childish mind I associated her with it.

"Don't you ever do that again, that's your

sister!" He told me. Clara Jean would get most of the whuppins though. She just wasn't really that humble back then.

Dad didn't usually say much. He would come in from work, we would have our time with him and he would go back to work. That pretty much seemed like the routine. I can still picture the clothes that he would wear to work. It was just the way that I pictured a man should look when he goes to work. He had his khakis and his shirt that we would have to iron for him. He had a hat that he wore that looked like a taxi driver's hat, with the rim that made it stand up. Making sure that his clothes were together was a part of my routine before I went to school. After school, I would have to come home and make sure that my father ate.

In the early fifties, when we were all still pretty young, Dad became sick. He worked at Walgreens drug store until he couldn't work anymore. Looking back, I think it was diabetes that my father suffered from, but back then people used the term dropsy and other things to explain it.

When my dad became so ill that he had to stop working, my mom stepped in to pick up the slack. She went to work at Fishburne Cleaners, which was up on Ross Avenue. She would walk up there, go to work and come back home. She worked as much as she could to try to fill that void. Those were big shoes to fill. She used to press clothes with the big steam machines that they had. I thought those were impressive when I was young. The simplest things can look amazing to you when you're young. There was a lady who was really nice to her that she struck up a friendship with and she lived right by the cleaners. My mom used to go over her house and eat lunch with her sometimes.

Mom would say, "Y'all make sure Willie eats something," and we would sit him up in the chair and make sure that he ate. He loved jello. I remember him always wanting me to put on the food, watch the beans, and make the cornbread. I learned fast when it came to cooking. I would whip up the cornbread with meal, salt, flour, sugar, baking powder and an egg and beat it real good before sliding it in the oven. I usually had to cook because my older sister, Clara Jean, didn't like to cook very much. She liked to clean and that was the area that she would handle. She would rather do that. So, together, we kept the house running. At that time, Buck, Florence, Phyllis and Roger were the young ones.

I remember one year around Christmas, my mom said, "They're not going to give Willie his check." I was around ten years old at this time. I suppose at that age it shouldn't have meant that much to me: at least not to the point where I should have believed that I could do something about it. Most parents would probably try to shelter their child from the economic realities of the household at that age. For whatever reason, she shared that with me.

When she told me that, I decided to take

action. Somehow, I felt like I had to do something, so, I did. I sat down and wrote a letter to the people at the Walgreens where he worked. I wrote, "My dad is real sick and Christmas is coming and we need our money." I finished up the letter in the best way that I could with my little communication skills at that age. I tried my best to express to them how badly we needed it. My mom found the letter and got on me about it, but I didn't let that stop me. I was stubborn like that.

At that age, I already knew how to go downtown on the bus. It cost five cents to ride the bus at that time. There was a bus that came right by Roseland that went directly down by Walgreens, so I didn't have to transfer. Sometimes, I would go and visit my grandmother on the bus and I would have to transfer to another bus, but to Walgreens, it was a direct shot.

At that time, when you got on the bus, you would see the arrows that told you where you had to sit according to your race. There was an arrow on top, pointing to the right, towards the bus driver, that simply read, "White." There was an arrow on the bottom, pointing to the left, towards the back, that simply read, "Colored." The word "colored" also appeared in great, big letters at the back of the bus to drive the point home, as if we could actually miss the arrows and the group of black people sitting in the back of the bus.

The line that separated black and white on the

bus was not some painted, permanent line that stretched across the floor of the bus. The line was determined by the people, the white people in particular, and it could move at any time. If we ever got on the bus, and a white person sat behind us, that meant we had to get up and move towards the back of the bus, somewhere behind them. We could never allow a white person to sit behind us. That was the line: the back of whatever white person was sitting the furthest towards the back of the bus.

We ended up learning to count and try to gauge how many seats would fill up when the white people started getting on the bus. What we would do is get on the bus and go sit in a place where we thought we wouldn't have to move, because it was so aggravating, and actually intimidating, to see a person get up and move because they were black. We didn't want to do that and be embarrassed, so we learned to be safe and sit in a place on the bus that would spare us that embarrassment. We did not want to get our feelings hurt by going through that time and time again.

Sometimes, they would even do it on purpose just to see us get up. We would already be sitting on the bus, and a white person would board and come and sit behind us, even though there were plenty of empty seats in front of us. The only seat on the entire bus that a black person could realistically claim was the very last seat on the bus, right beneath the word "Colored." In 1956, they finally passed the law that allowed black people to sit anywhere they wanted to on the bus. We were so happy that a lot of us rode the bus and sat directly behind the bus driver just because we could.

Sometimes, my dad would take me to work with him, pin his check under my skirt, put me back on the bus, and send me home from Walgreens to take it to my mother. So, I didn't have a problem getting back there on my own. I took it down to the store manager, and I had my friend with me: a boy named Bubba.

I told him, "I'm trying to go downtown. You wanna come?" I knew where to get off the bus, and where to get back on the bus. I also took Floyd along with me. When I entered the store, I had the letter in my hand and a man recognized me right away.

Referring to the letter, he asked, "What's this little Mopping?"

"I need to give you this letter for my dad, because he's sick," I told him.

I gave him the letter, and I caught the bus back home.

"Don't you ever do that again," my mom told me when she found out I had actually gone down there. Then she smiled at me and said, "You're so amazing." She couldn't help but be tickled by the whole ordeal. I think it made her proud to see that I did it, even though I had no business doing it.

"Well, Dad is sick," I explained, "and he can't work, so we needed some toys for Christmas." They ended up buying us some skates and other stuff for Christmas, and they brought my mother her money. A man who worked there brought about 25 dollars, which was a pretty good amount of money back then. Besides the skates, they gave us some little rag dolls and small toys. I was pretty brave back then, and in that case, it paid off. You could never stop me from speaking up if I thought something needed to be said, and that's something that has never changed.

My mom was a great seamstress, so she would sew presents for us at Christmas time. My uncle, Andrew Jackson, would always bring us a box with presents in it like dolls, skates, and trucks for the boys, and we would be waiting on him to send it to us. Before my dad got sick, he would bring us some things from Walgreens. That stopped once he became ill.

We would cook up a nice Christmas dinner, and I always had to help Mom with that. I enjoyed it, so it wasn't like it was a chore. It was fun for me. It was exciting to be responsible for helping to prepare the meal that everyone was looking forward to.

Sometimes people would give us food to help us out, but Mama always managed somehow: that was a given. She was going to make a way. She showed me how to clean the greens and prepare everything. She showed Sandra one time and she didn't clean them good, so she threw the water on her and whupped her and we had a good laugh about that for a long time, ha!

"These greens are gritty!" she screamed at her while Sandra stood there with water dripping off her.

At that age, there's only so much I could comprehend, so I didn't realize everything that was really going on, but I knew we didn't have any money while Mama was trying to get us ready for Christmas. I think she might have been a little sick already at that point. Looking back now, I can clearly see how hard things were for them. It just didn't seem that way back then and that's what hurts me. I wish I could have done more. Now, it makes me question how they made it sometimes.

They really made sure that they put an emphasis on making us good people. They couldn't guarantee we'd be well-off financially, but they could control whether or not we were good people, and they put their all into it. Growing up without a lot of material things allows you to see that those things are not always promised, but you can always be a good person no matter how much money you have in the bank. Both my mother and my father were big on that.

As Dad's condition got worse, we had to do more things to help pick up the slack and take care of him. My brothers would help me clean him up.

"You better clean him up good," Mama would tell us. We had a little tin tub that we would fill up with soap and water. I would still have to make sure that we fed him. He always wanted me to be the one who fed him because I would take my time and not try to rush him to finish. One day, a boy was meddling with Daddy, and I beat him up good over it.

"That old man sitting on that porch every day. What's wrong with him?" He taunted. Actually, he really said a lot more than that. I chased him down, caught him and gave him a good beating. Kids can be cruel as we all know. They had no idea what we were going through though. Dad used to sit on the porch just to get some fresh air and then we would bring him back in the house. We had to pad the bed and then lift him up in it. We had to get his bed pan when he had to use the bathroom. He couldn't breathe too well so he started sleeping in his chair instead of the bed.

It's funny how people can remember certain things about you that you never remember yourself. Judy and Fred both said that I used to just break out and cry sometimes and they never knew why. I don't remember crying so openly in public like that, but if they both say it, it must be true. It's amazing how we can block things out of our minds. They had no way of knowing all of the situations I was going through at home that would make me cry, such as when my parents were sick. What was I supposed to do? Go to school and tell them my parents were sick?

One day, we were in the living room and my mother was combing Florence's hair. Dad was in the chair but he was kind of slumped over and he had been sitting that way for a while.

"Carolyn, touch Willie," Mama told me.

"No," I started to protest.

"You heard what I said!" she snapped. I touched him and his arm just fell.

"Oh my God!" she started screaming. I grabbed the phone and dialed 7-4-4-1-1-1-1, which was the emergency number at the time. They hadn't simplified it to 9-1-1 yet. It was on Memorial Day. The ambulance came, and a lot of people from the neighborhood came by to see what was going on. When they covered up his face, it made me lose it.

"Don't do that, don't do that to him!" I told them.

"Willie's dead, I know he's dead!" Mama screamed. Once they pronounced him dead, we started preparing for the burial. Even though he was sick for a long time, the end still seemed sudden. When you haven't dealt with the death of someone that close to you, you don't know what to expect. In your mind, you can convince yourself that it will just continue to go on that way.

My father was such a consistent part of our lives that it left a huge void when he passed. It was hard for all of us to wrap our minds around. He had laid the foundation for what our lives should be like, and now he wasn't there anymore. I had to spend as much time around my mother as I could. At that point, Mama started going down as well. A lot of married couples who have been together for so long tend to do that. When one goes, the other starts to go down immediately. We buried our dad at Lincoln Memorial Cemetery. Peoples Funeral Home handled the arrangements. It was 1955.

3 THE WOMAN OF THE HOUSE

As the event ends, Ms. Price exits the banquet hall and heads back through the adjacent room to leave. She sees former Cowboy Nate Newton, who hosted the event, coming out behind her.

"Nate Newton!" *He approaches her and she hugs him tightly.* "My boy Nate!" *she laughs.*

During the Cowboys' dynasty of the 1990's, Newton was one of the team's biggest and best players. Standing 6'3" and more than 330 pounds at his peak, he was a big man in a game of giants. He was an integral part of the Cowboys' celebrated offensive line that provided protection for quarterback Troy Aikman, and opened huge holes for running back Emmitt Smith.

"How you doing?" *he asks with his arm around her.*

"I'm great darling, how are you?"

"I'm doing good."

"When I used to see you at training camp, I wore you out didn't I?"

"Naw, you didn't wear me out. We got used to you real quick, girl," Newton replies.

"I know you did," says Ms. Price. "You are looking so good Nate, you look like a basketball player instead of a football player." Newton laughs at that description. He is much slimmer than during his playing days.

"Y'all be good. God bless you." He gives Ms. Price another hug before walking away.

"Love you Nate."

"Love you too."

As Newton heads in the opposite direction, Ms. Price, along with her friends Cynthia and Earline, continue towards the car to make it to the next destination. Cynthia is a Cowboys fan from Memphis, and Earline is a fan from San Antonio. Ms. Price met both of them as a result of a mutual love for The Cowboys.

As is the case with most people, if Ms. Price really likes you, and trusts you, you're in. Her generosity is limitless. Both Cynthia and Earline are in town this weekend for the game against the Lions.

Ms. Price is now moving at the speed reserved for when she's trying to make it somewhere, and is oblivious to other people around her in the hallway. She does not see Fox television personality Pam Oliver walking directly towards her trying to get her attention.

"Ms. Price, hey how are you?" Pam is all the way in Ms. Price's face with her hand on her shoulder before she realizes who's speaking to her.

"Oh my God! Look at my girl. Ms. Fox herself," she hugs Pam. As Cynthia and Earline excitedly greet Pam and *began to speak, Ms. Price playfully cuts them off. "She's talking to Ms. Price, would y'all hush?" she tells them as they laugh.*

"You're doing the game tomorrow?" she asks Pam.

"Yes, I am," Pam replies.

"Come and stand in front of Ms. Price. Do y'all know who this beautiful woman is? Take this picture. I want a good picture with Pam. I want my star to show."

"Which one?" Pam asks sarcastically.

"I'm so proud of you," she tells Pam. "You know I'm proud of you too, I just love you," Pam replies.

"Well thank you."

"You've got energy to burn. I want energy like yours," Pam says.

"You got it!" They share one more hug before departing.

"Bye baby, do the game good tomorrow. I'll see you there."

"Oh, I will."

"Just say 'we got Ms. Price on the sideline cheering them on,' that's all you have to do."

"That's exactly what I'll say," Pam laughs.

"Do you know I was about to pass you up? I didn't even notice you," says Ms. Price.

"Well, I wasn't passing you up. I saw you. I couldn't miss you," says Pam.

"GO GET EM! See you tomorrow."

"See you then."

When high school rolled around, I began attending Booker T. Washington High School. At

55

Booker T. Washington, we were active in a lot of different ways. We had adults and role models who truly made us feel like we could do whatever we put our minds to. They didn't allow us to get caught up in the mentality of what was around us. They didn't let us place any limitations or ceilings on what we could be. Our principal, J.L. Patton, used to get on the microphone and say, "this is a great school and a great community!"

He used to always say that at the end of his morning announcements, and we believed him when he said it. Looking back, you'd think, "this is not a great community, this is the ghetto!" But we didn't think like that. He didn't allow us to think like that. The people in the school and in the community were what made it great, and he made sure that we knew it. The school was about ten blocks from the projects and we used to walk to and from school. In those days we still had prayer at school every morning before class started. We also had devotion, just like we would have at church.

I participated in a lot of activities in high school, but I had asthma, so sometimes it made it harder because I would be sick. I loved being a cheerleader. Judy was on the drill team. We used to perform at football games. Sometimes the games would be at a place called Dal-Hi Stadium: they later changed the name to Cobb Stadium. When we would have our games there on the colored nights, they would sell us French fries but we didn't get ketchup to put on our fries like white people did on any other night: they gave us mustard. Can you imagine that?

In school, there are some teachers that you remember more than others and they tend to shape the way that you remember your time in school. Mrs. Massey was one of those teachers who really inspired me. Mrs. Ross, my typing and journalism teacher, Mr. McKenzie, my music teacher, Ms. Davis, my history teacher, and Mr. Gulley, my science teacher were all great teachers. They always wanted me to go to college. They encouraged me every chance that they got, but my sisters and brothers needed me, and I never allowed myself to lose sight of that.

Ms. Ross really inspired the interest that I had in journalism. I remember one time she helped me with an article that I wrote to submit to the school paper. I didn't know how they would feel about it, but they really liked it. They printed the article in the school paper. That gave me confidence to think that I could actually get better and better and pursue that as my career. From that point on, I wanted to go to college to become a journalist. I planned to go to Prairie View A&M to pursue a degree in journalism. I took a tour to the campus and everything. Life has a way of changing up your plans though.

Prairie View A&M was the first state supported college for black people in Texas. It was a few hours away from Dallas, closer to Houston. Of course, this was during the time when the colleges were still segregated. Those of us who wanted to attend college back then all wanted to go to Prairie View. There had been a handful of students admitted to other colleges, starting with Texas Western College, which is now UTEP, but we still didn't see that as a realistic option.

When my teachers found out that my mother was sick, and that I was taking care of my family, they would do little things to help me.

"Mopping, I know you have to take care of your brothers and sisters, but don't you think for one minute about dropping out of school," Ms. Ross told me. All of them just really stepped in and encouraged me on so many levels. Most of the other kids would get picked up from school by their parents, but since I didn't have anyone, they would get me things like ice cream sandwiches, and other things that you would expect someone's parents to get for them.

I was really blessed to have teachers that were compassionate and saw an opportunity to make a difference in my life. I had such a weight on my shoulders from helping my mom run the household at such an early age, and in any small way that they could, they tried to lift some of that off me.

We called Mr. McKenzie "Prop." He actually married Ms. Ross, but that was much later on. He was a great teacher also and had a big impact on my life. He taught music. The kids from Booker T. were smart overall. We basically had a year under our belt of college-level education by the time we graduated. A lot of students went on to Prairie View A&M and stood out because they were very well-prepared. A lot of times when I was sick with my asthma, I would try to use it an excuse. Mr. McKenzie wasn't having it, and would never allow it on his watch.

"Mopping, you're just going to have to find a way to get your lesson," he'd say.

Sometimes my mom would say, "Carolyn, come over and eat lunch with me today on your break." I would walk down there from Booker T. Washington to eat lunch with her during our lunch period, and then go back in time for my next class.

I didn't realize that she had already begun to get sick. She didn't mention it to us. She didn't want to put that weight on us.

She would call and say, "Come meet me and walk me home," and I would walk about a mile down to Fishburne and walk home with her. Looking back, she had to be suffering from arthritis too. Again, you don't really know what the specific condition might be when you're young, you just get used to it.

Floyd would say, "I don't want to go up there," because he was embarrassed. Sometimes, the kids would laugh at us because of her condition and how we had to help her walk home. She would have to actually lean on us while we walked home sometimes. Looking back, I don't know why she didn't get a cane, but we became the substitute for having a cane. When one of the children would say something, I would yell, "You got one more time to say something. Come on down here, I'll beat you…"

"Carolyn, stop it," she would be the voice of reason. I would then go tell Clara Jean because she liked to fight, and she was good at it. She would tear people up! Sandra and Clara Jean both liked to fight.

They would go back and handle the situation and put people in their places: quickly. Despite everything she was going through, and everything she had to take care of with us, she was still always trying to help out other children as well.

Eventually, she became sicker and couldn't work, so she drew my father's social security and we lived off that. Of course, that wasn't a lot of money to live on for a family the size of ours, but like most of the other things that were thrown our way, we adjusted to it and kept going. Mom managed to buy us a lot of nice things. We may not have had everything we wanted, but we had what we needed. One time, she got a check for a lump sum of around eight or nine hundred dollars. That was a lot of money at the time. Bread wasn't even 20 cents a loaf. She took us to Sears and let us treat ourselves to some really nice things.

After a while, she was in and out of the hospital. She would go and get treated, stay a little while, and then come back home. I had the responsibility of waking up and making sure that the kids had their clothes ready for school and that they had eaten something.

Pastor Jackson was always coming by our house to see us and give us updates about our mother's condition once she became sick. I didn't see it that way then, but looking back, he had become the mediator between the doctors and our family. Being the man that he was, I suppose they trusted him to guide us through that difficult time. It was a wise choice.

When her condition worsened to the point where she was really near the end, Rev. Jackson came by our house and told us that he had been called out to the hospital to see my mother. When he got there, we were all sitting in the living room and he told us what kind of condition that she was in.

"Children, I'm sorry to have to tell you this," he said, "but your mother has leukemia and she may not live much longer."

"That's not true," I told him.

"Carolyn, you're something else," he chuckled sympathetically.

"It can't be true," I explained. "Daddy is already dead, and Jesus wouldn't do that. We wouldn't have anybody to take care of us." He just smiled at my line of reasoning.

"Jesus wouldn't take her away from us," I continued. Of course, it wasn't that simple.

On Halloween of that year, she was in the hospital and she called and told me, "I need you to come out here and talk to me so I can let you know some things to do."

"Yes ma'am," I told her. When I went to visit her, she actually began telling me things that she needed me to do when she was gone. She went down a mental checklist of all the things I needed to know to run the house properly.

"You're going to have to grow up Carolyn," she said. "You're going to have to take care of your sisters and brothers." I just silently nodded my head as she spoke.

"You know they're not going to help you right?" she referred to my older siblings. "You're going to have to grow up. And I don't want those people putting all of that lipstick on me," she told me.

What in the world is she talking about? "Ok, mama," I told her. I was listening, but my mind didn't want to accept what she was trying to tell me.

"Sandra y'all, we have to go home," I told the others. As we walked home, kids were out throwing eggs and all the crazy stuff they do on Halloween. That next morning, we received a call.

"Y'all need to get back out here because your mother is not doing well," a hospital staff member told me. When I got there and walked into the room, I noticed that the nurse had my class ring on her finger. My mom was wearing my class ring when she went into the hospital. I realized she was gone.

"Where's my mama?" I snapped at her. By that time, Clara Jean had made it to the hospital and she was screaming and hollering. Floyd got there and he was pretty much doing the same. They were really acting up. They had to let them see her in order to quiet them down.

"Come with me," the doctor told us. He allowed them to go back. I didn't move.

"You don't wanna see her?" they asked.

"No," I shook my head. I didn't want to see her like that. I had already seen her the day before when she was still alive.

Sandra was really sad because Mama died on her birthday. I was only 17 years old, and I had to become not only an adult, but a guardian for my siblings. I told my teachers that I wouldn't be able to attend college anymore since my mother had passed and I had to take care of the house. They encouraged me to at least study a trade since I couldn't go away to college.

I went to Mountain View Community College and got a few courses in, but I couldn't go away because I knew that I had to be there for my brothers and sisters, no matter what. I would never allow anything to stand in the way of that: not even a college degree. If my mother had lived longer, I'm sure I would have gone on to college, and there's no telling how things would have turned out. But I had to grow up fast, and that dream died with her.

There were some nights that I didn't get any sleep while I was watching over my younger brothers and sisters. At times, I was up until three or four in the morning, dozing off in a chair, because I was worried about them.

I was worried about whether or not my

brothers, sisters and I would all be able to stay together. It wasn't a guaranteed thing. It was something I had to fight for. I was the oldest in the house, but I wasn't eighteen yet. While Mama was sick, a woman named Hazel had started coming around. She would come sometimes and sit with Mama, and we didn't think much of it. She said she was related to my mother, and maybe she was, but we didn't know how.

Shortly after Mama passed, she came back. Because I was not legally an adult yet, Hazel took my younger siblings from me. She only wanted to keep them because of the social security money she could get as their guardian. My older siblings were out living their own lives. Clara Jean was pretty much just out there, and Floyd had gotten with an older lady and moved in with her. He was only nineteen and she was around thirty-five.

4 FOOTBALL IN DALLAS

Ms. Price and her friends are standing in the lobby of the Gaylord Hotel where the Cowboys stay on the night before the game. Like most of the other events, it looks like a gathering of extended family with countless people dressed in Cowboys' jerseys and other attire. Ms. Price is holding court while an obnoxious heckler seeks her attention. It's rare for someone to bother her in this way, but this particular person has had too much alcohol and is a bit out of control. He yells some incoherent babble towards Ms. Price and her friends.

"I didn't understand a word you said. What did you say?" asks Ms. Price.

"E-A-G-L-E-S!" He punctuated every letter with a resounding clap of his hands as he yelled.

"Is something wrong with you?"

"Hell yeah!" he screams.

"Don't you use profanity," she scolds him. "Do you think we're looking for some fans? We're America's Team, we don't need any fans."

"E-A-G-L-E-S, let's go!"

"We're not looking for any fans. You're wasting time over here."

A Cowboys fan who's been standing by watching slides up to introduce himself.

"Don't worry about him. This is like meeting a movie star to me."

"Why thank you! What's your name?"

"Timmy." The young man replies and the drunk fan drifts into the background seeking other targets to antagonize.

"Nice to meet you."

"I see you on TV all the time. I love your spirit."

"Well, I have so much fun, honey. I wish you knew just how much fun I have," she tells the man.

"Well, we want to be just like you."

"You can be. Just be a true blue Cowboys fan. TRUE BLUE!" Her voice bounces off the high ceilings and reverberates through the room. *"GO GET 'EM! Whoo, I be so fired up!"* Scattered laughter emanates from the small group of fans who've gathered around Ms. Price.

"This is great. This is my first time here," the man reveals.

"Oh, where are you from?"

"Baltimore."

"And you came down just for the game? So, you're a true blue Cowboys fan?"

"Oh yeah, I love the Cowboys! Ms. Price is in the house!" The man pulls his phone out and holds it in the air to take a picture with Ms. Price. She smiles for the picture before finishing up the conversation.

"God bless you honey, y'all always pray for me ok?"

"Oh, most definitely."

"I'm having the time of my life," says Ms. Price.

"Well, I'm with you. This is like heaven getting the chance to come and see it like this. I don't even want to leave Dallas now, but I gotta go back to Baltimore," says the man.

"Well, let me tell you something. Get on my Facebook...I don't even know it by heart. I tell you what, let me give you my phone number." She recites her number and he programs it into the phone. "Call me so you can get on my Facebook, ok?"

"Ok, I'll do that."

"Y'all let's move it!" She walks away and her group walks with her, with a couple of extra members now in tow tagging along through the hotel lobby.

I was around sixteen years old when the Dallas Cowboys started playing football in the National Football League. All we had was a baseball team at the time.

One day, my brother said, "Carolyn, we're getting a football team!"

"Really? Wow!" It was exciting to hear. Then, he came back and told me that we actually had two teams that were going to play in Dallas, and that was unbelievable. The Dallas Texans started playing the same year in the American Football League, or AFL, which was a new rival league to the NFL, but The Cowboys quickly became our favorite.

My dad used to like baseball. That's what pretty

much got me into sports in the first place. Sometimes, I got a chance to go with him to the baseball games. From there, my interest grew, and I just really began to enjoy watching sports. I had no way of knowing that the Cowboys would even come into existence, and certainly not that they would become so popular. My girlfriends used to want to go shopping, and I would be the one sitting there just wanting to turn on the TV and watch sports. I ran track, and I was a cheerleader and that may have had something to do with it. Overall, I didn't want to do a lot of ripping and running. I just wanted to go home and watch the games.

In the beginning, there weren't a lot of big crowds, or sellouts, or anything like that. There were just people scattered throughout the stadium. Later in the 60's, when the Cowboys began to win, that changed. The end zones used to be filled with all the black people because that is where the cheap seats were. All up the sidelines was where the white people were, and the contrast made it look like a big painted cover pulled over the stadium.

The price of admission for the least expensive tickets was one dollar at the time. The team played at The Cotton Bowl stadium. They actually shared the stadium with the Dallas Texans for the first few seasons. The games attracted all different classes of people, but especially those with money. A dollar wasn't a small, insignificant amount of money if you were poor. The location of the Cotton Bowl caused some problems because it was in a poor neighborhood. It was in a neighborhood where a lot of the residents couldn't afford to go to the games.

As usual, neighborhoods with a lot of poor people often had problems with crime. A lot of people with money like doctors, lawyers and all other types of professional people would bring their families to the games. In order to get to the stadium, they had to park their cars and walk right through the heart of the ghetto. They would park in a bunch of strange places like people's yards and side streets and they were put in a position to become victims of the ghetto. That's what happened in a lot of cases.

A lot of people had their cars broken into and had items stolen from them. People were threatened coming through the neighborhood, and had their children exposed to a lot of foul language. It became a situation where the team owner and others in the community realized that it wasn't the safest neighborhood for the season ticket holders. There was a sense of urgency to get the Cowboys out of that neighborhood and into their own stadium. They began building Texas Stadium in the suburb of Irving, and the team began playing there in 1971.

The Cotton Bowl was in the Fair Park area, which was the home of the State Fair of Texas. The State Fair was the biggest event going, and maybe the single biggest thing that we looked forward to every year. The fair began in September every year, and lasted for about three weeks. It didn't last three weeks for us though.

For us, the fair was only one day: the only day when black people were allowed to attend the fair. They called it Negro Achievement Day. It was originally called "Colored People's Day" and had begun back in the late 1800's. The people who ran the fair explained the purpose of Negro Achievement Day as a way to recognize the accomplishments and progress of black people in the state of Texas and around the United States as a whole. All we knew was that it was the one day that we were allowed to go to the fair, and every year, we couldn't wait.

Like the rest of Texas, and the United States as a whole, the history of the State Fair was filled with events that were common at the time, but were very embarrassing later on to people in an integrated society. I found out later on that back in 1923, the fair had even hosted a Ku Klux Klan day where thousands of new Klan members were sworn in right there at the fairgrounds.

I remember people protesting against the discrimination around the late 1950's and early 1960's outside of the gates. As in other parts of the south, the Civil Rights Movement was in full swing, and people in Dallas were a part of it. With the State Fair being such a big event, it was a symbol of the segregation that people were fighting against, and many people turned their attention to the fair as the target of their protests.

Later on, the word Negro was dropped from the

name, and the day designated for black people was simply known as Achievement Day. By 1961, the courts had ordered all institutions to desegregate, and the mayor at the time, R. L. Thornton, announced that the State Fair would fall in line with the court order. Negro Achievement Day officially ended in 1961, but it was not until 1967 that segregation ended in all of the attractions at the fair.

Long before that though, we just had our one day. On Negro Achievement day, black people from all over Texas, little country towns and all, would make their way to Dallas to attend the fair. Black people came by the busload and enjoyed every minute of it. They gave us passes that allowed us to ride the bus for free, and they gave us tickets to get into the fair for free also. For that small window of time, the other things didn't matter. We wouldn't miss it for anything in the world. We didn't focus on the fact that it was the only day out of several weeks that we could go. We just looked at it as a day for us.

We looked forward to hanging out with not only our friends, but a whole bunch of people that we might never see again. They pretty much had the same type of rides, games and food that they have nowadays at the fair, just less of them. We had no complaints about whether we had enough rides, or anything like that. We were going to ride them over and over like it was our very first time.

We tried to go as early as we could to pack as much fun into that day as possible. We made the most of the time that we had. We would always make sure we were looking our best. Looking back now, it's funny how we dressed up to go: we didn't dress down and get comfortable like you might imagine for an outdoor event like that. Instead of wearing some tennis shoes and blue jeans, we dressed in our Sunday's best because we were so excited. We looked more like we were going to church than to a fair.

There was a sense of pride attached to it. All of the girls would make sure that their hair was done, boys would have their hair cut, and shoes would be shined. It wasn't about trying to wear some expensive brand-name clothes. That didn't exist even if we had the money. We just wanted to be really neat and well-groomed when we showed up. Even on that day though, we still got reminded of what was going on in the world around us. It was common to be walking down the street on the way to the fair and have someone pass by calling us niggers. They would say, "It's nigger day at the fair!"

The Cowboys were not a good team at first, but it was exciting just to have a team. My sister Sandra loved the Cowboys and was a big football fan like me. One year I took her for her birthday and she got into a serious argument with somebody for talking about the Cowboys. She loved the Cowboys and would get really angry when people would tease her or talk about them. No one ever teases me though.

If they say anything to me it's something more like, "Ms. Price, I'm sure sorry about that loss," but to meddle me about it? No. I don't know if they're afraid or if it's just respect. I really don't know why, but if they say something negative I'll just usually say, "Excuse me?" They know to go on about their business.

A lot of us were football fans. When we were young, my brother Willie played football. He had big dreams of making it to the NFL. He didn't get to go far in it, but he played for years. My friend Fred played football back then also.

Willie came to me one day at school talking about rumors that the teams were leaving town. We didn't know the details, or what any of it meant, so it seemed really big in in our minds.

"They say they gon' get rid of our football teams," he told me. For a while, we were worried about whether or not they were going to take the Cowboys away from us. We were anxiously watching our little television, well actually, our big television, because this was back when they were size of a big old cabinet.

We heard that they flipped a coin and the Hunt family, who owned the Texans, took them to Kansas City. We got to keep the Cowboys in Dallas. To us, that was a relief, because the Cowboys were the team that we liked better anyway even though we still cheered for the Texans. Thank the Lord! If that star would have been in Kansas City, I don't know how we would have been able to live with ourselves. We were so dedicated to Dallas that we would still pull for the Texans, even after they became the Kansas City Chiefs, unless they had to play the Cowboys. They were in a different league so we didn't have to bother with them a whole lot.

I remember we had come up with some kind of gray tops and blue clothes, and we dressed up to celebrate the Cowboys staying in Dallas. I used to dream about the players like they were actually around me and it would seem so vivid. I had no idea that later I would be blessed to be around so many players. I ended up meeting a lot of the Cowboys who were heroes to me when I was young. Back then, I would dream about players like Rayfield Wright and "Dandy" Don Meredith.

1966 was the year that the team finally broke through and had a winning season. That year, the team played against the Green Bay Packers in the NFL Championship. The winner would go on to play in the first Super Bowl, but nobody really knew what that was. It wasn't even called that back then. That was looked at as more a novelty, with the NFL champion playing against the champion of the AFL. What really mattered to us was The NFL Championship.

We watched on television as Green Bay won by a touchdown, 34-27 and went on to Super Bowl I, which was called the AFL-NFL World Championship Game that year. Ironically, the team they played and defeated in that game was the Kansas City Chiefs, our old Dallas Texans. They got both of our teams back to back.

The first player on the team that I met in person was Cornell Green. I remember it like it was yesterday. His story was unique because he didn't even play football in college. He used to play basketball, and in those days, The Cowboys had to be creative with the way they got players because they were still new and they didn't have much talent. During their first season, they didn't even participate in the draft. They had to basically fill up the team with players that other teams didn't want. They got a tip from somebody about how great of an athlete he was and they tried him at football. He turned out to be great at it. He played defensive back and made it to the Pro Bowl a bunch of times. He played for the team well into the 70's and became one of the best Cowboys of that time.

From the time they came into existence, I wanted to go to every game, but it wasn't until much later when I could afford to buy my own tickets and go whenever I felt like it. I never could understand why when I would go to the stadium and come back, I would always be so relaxed. Thank you Jesus. It became therapy for me. There always seemed to be so much going on in my life that I needed an escape, I suppose. I didn't plan it that way, but that's what it became: a wonderful escape. Sometimes I would leave the game and go straight to the hospital because one of my brothers or sisters was sick, or there was some other family situation that I had to tend to.

Early in 1961, I went to visit my dad's brother, my Uncle Andrew, in Paris, Texas. I suddenly had a need to get away. I had been spending quite a bit of time with a guy I liked. We always had fun when we were together. He was a really cool guy, but he showed me pretty early on that he wasn't the type I could get too serious about, because he wasn't serious himself. By the time I figured it out, I discovered that I was in a situation that wouldn't be so easy to walk away from: I was pregnant. I knew that the father of the baby was not the type of person who was going to be around to be with the child and he had shown that. I found out that he already had a couple of other kids at the time. I felt alone. I was depressed and ashamed, and I just needed to get away.

Clara Jean came to look after the house while I was away. Hazel still had my four younger siblings with her at her house. That was another thing that was weighing on me. I was upset because I was still fighting to get them back. Sandra stayed with Clara Jean. Floyd was still with the woman who he was living with. One day, my sister Florence called me from Hazel's house.

"Carolyn, she went and bought her kids a bunch of clothes and stuff with that money," she said. "We just sitting here wearing the same thing over and over."

"Don't worry about it baby, I'll get y'all back home," I told her. "That's ok." It wasn't ok though. It was really bad and it was extremely stressful to see that this woman was just able to step in and take advantage of our family to get my father's social security money for her own personal gain. So, the entire situation was just really weighing heavily on me: both being pregnant and trying to fight the juvenile department to get my brothers and sisters back. I thought it was the right time to get away and hopefully get a little peace of mind.

It was not too long before Thanksgiving, so I decided to spend the holiday with them and then come back. I was speaking to my aunt about it.

"Well, do you want to just stay down here?" she asked.

"No, thanks," I told her. "I still want to go back home."

"Ok, well just stay here awhile and get yourself together," she replied. "Have you seen a doctor?"

I already had my appointments and everything else I needed set up at Parkland Hospital in Dallas, so I was preparing to return home. Before I could, I started dilating and the pains started. They told me that she would probably come around New Year's Day. I was hurting really bad. The pain was really intense. They allowed me to go through it, and I stayed in labor and suffered. Finally, just when they decided to take her, she came.

My daughter Charmayne was born on January 6th. My aunt would not let me leave. She would not let me do anything. They would take Charmayne shopping and other places with them, but I couldn't go. She insisted that I rest. She made sure I was healthy and didn't have any setbacks. They really took care of me. I ended up staying there until March. After that, I headed back home to Clara Jean and Sandra. Now, bringing a baby into the situation obviously made it even harder. It was only by the grace of God that I made it through.

When I came back, Clara Jean moved back to her house, and I used to go by and spend time with her there. One day, when I went over there she had company. There was a man there to see her and he had a friend with him. The friend's name was Willie Price.

Willie was a pretty tall guy, about 6'1" or 6'2" with a slender build and broad shoulders. He had a smooth, dark-brown complexion. That day, I came in, stayed awhile and I left. He conveniently was there again the next time I went over.

"He said you're going to be his wife," Clara Jean said.

"Is he crazy? What is he talking about?" I asked.

Eventually, we began dating and hit it off. He was really nice to me at that point and he won me over. I felt safe with him, and I fell in love with him. After we dated for a good while, he wanted me to come and live with him.

"You spend so much time back and forth here with me, you might as well just move in," he said.

"I can't just stay with you or nothing like that because my mom raised us in church, and I can't do that," I told him. His answer to that was marriage. We went to the courthouse and made it official. He had an aunt named Beulah, and she went with us to the courthouse to be the witness.

I wish things went as smoothly with the rest of his family. My mother-in-law was very, very mean to me. I think a lot of people took advantage of the fact that I didn't have parents to call on for help with certain things. I couldn't call Mama or Daddy, so in so many ways, I was alone and vulnerable. Everyone wants to feel like they have someone that can protect them in situations where it's needed and I didn't feel that. I was left without that. I had become that for other people, but I didn't have anyone to fill that need for me. The person who should have been that person was my husband, and it wasn't long before he was one of the people hurting me. I was just out there wading in the water trying to stay afloat.

A big part of the problem was that my ex-husband was taking care of his mother and everyone around her financially, and when we got married, he supported our household, which is what he was supposed to do as a husband. That caused them to resent me as if I was taking something away from them, instead of being happy about the fact that he had found a wife. They would come over to our home and take his clothes and other belongings out of the house. It was horrible. My mother-in-law had remarried and she was no longer with my husband's father. She would actually send her husband over to our house on Willie's payday to get money from him!

"Hey, how you doing Carolyn?" He would just casually come through the door as if it was the most normal thing. "Where's Willie?" How do you go over to your stepson's house at that age expecting him to support you?

My husband was a very, very hard worker. That's something that I can never take away from him despite the other things he did. He worked in construction. He worked hard and he brought the money home. I took the money that he brought home and I made it work for us. He liked the Cowboys, but he didn't like them as much as I did. I was still there every Sunday faithfully. They just could not believe that I wanted to go as much as I did. When I got home from church, my husband would start to act ignorant, because he knew what was next.

"Y'all going out to that stadium, huh?" he would ask. He was nervous, I guess. I was pretty and well-built. Maybe, in his mind, he feared that a Cowboys' player would try to steal me away, ha! I don't really know what he thought.

I always knew that the Cowboys were a great franchise because of the extra attention they got from the media. They're supposed to be impartial and talk about everybody the same, but let's be serious: how can you do that when the Cowboys are involved? Legendary television personalities like Howard Cosell on Monday Night Football and John Madden when he went to TV, even though they weren't supposed to make a bigger deal of them, you could tell that it made their job more fun when the Cowboys were playing. That's not just me saying that.

Monday Night Football came on television for the first time in 1970. People are used to it now, but it was a really odd concept at the time because everyone was used to Sunday being the day for football. I loved "Dandy" Don Meredith on Monday Night Football just as much as I did as a player for our Cowboys. Whenever a team was getting beat and it was obvious they were not coming back, he used to sing that song, "turn out the lights...the parties over," and I would sing right along with him.

I had a special chair, and I would just sit and watch them. I liked the analyst Jimmy "the Greek" Snyder back then because he always took up for Dallas. This was long before he lost his job over his comments about African-Americans. We were very much into it, and we stayed that way consistently.

I would always come straight home for Monday Night Football, especially if Dallas was playing. I used to dream that I had a really big house and I would be in there cooking for the Cowboys. That's how obsessed I was with them, ha!

I used to tell my husband, "I dreamed the Cowboys were over here," and he'd say, "Girl, if you don't get out of my face! What is wrong with you?"

The way that his mother treated me hurt me more than it probably would have under normal circumstances because I didn't have my own parents.

When my siblings got married, for the most part, they were very close to their in-laws. They were able to bond with them to help fill the void that we had from losing our parents.

My in-laws never knew how much they hurt me because I didn't wear my emotions on my sleeve in that way. I would hold it in, but when I got home, I would cry. If their aim was to try to get the best of me, I never gave them the satisfaction of knowing that they got to me. My mother-in-law was alright sometimes, but for the most part, she was something else to deal with. My sisters-in-law were alright. We weren't very close, but we got along.

My brother and my older sister were very protective of me, so that would cause tension between them and my in-laws. I can't say it was all terrible, but as a whole it was a bad situation, and another one that I had to endure instead of enjoy.

By this time, my brothers and sisters were all doing pretty well for themselves. Willie Harold worked at Neiman's for years with Phyllis. They were building a shopping center in the 60's and a lot of people went out there and got jobs. They became porters, stockgirls and things like that. Phyllis became a salesperson in hosiery and Buck stayed down below and worked as a stock boy.

Gary Floyd went down to the gas company as a porter, and he started messing around with the computers while he was there. Of course, computers weren't like they are now. They were manual, with the cords, and the little holes in them. There was a guy who saw what he had done and would always call him in to help out. He would get on there and he just took to it as if he had gone to school for it. Like I said, back in school, he may have struggled with certain things, but there's no substitute for God-given ability. He got hired on and actually became the first black computer operator in Dallas.

Still fairly early in my marriage, I was standing out in front of our house one day, and I had Charmayne out there with me. She was still a small baby. There was this guy that was a friend to my sister-in-law, my husband's sister, and he was a very playful guy. Besides being a friend of the family, he was also a truck driver. His route would bring him into our neighborhood and he used to stop by our house to visit.

One day when he was out on his route he pulled up and he said, "You better not be going downtown, your president just got shot."

Because of the type of person he was, I didn't pay him any attention. Even though joking about President John F. Kennedy getting killed would seem odd, he was the type to always crack jokes and play around. Of course, I soon found out that he was not playing at all. I couldn't believe that the President of the United States had been shot, and especially right here in Dallas. It was devastating.

In so many people's eyes, he represented hope. People looked at him as the person who would truly make things different. We had great civil rights leaders like Martin Luther King, but it was people like John F. Kennedy who they were trying to reach to make the change. We needed someone on the inside who cared, and we truly believed that he did.

I was actually about to head downtown right before I heard the news. Had I left ten or fifteen minutes earlier, I would have gotten trapped down there in the chaos like so many other people. They had shut down the streets and no one could get out. I was very hurt because I really looked up to him and supported him at the time. When he had first been elected, I didn't get a chance to vote for him because I wasn't quite old enough, but I followed everything closely and knew that I would have voted for him.

They had rushed him to the same hospital where my mother and father passed. It was like it brought those memories back to the surface for me. It put a damper on everything and I was just really hurt. The cloud is still hanging over the city. The same way people in Memphis talk about Dr. King being killed there, it never fully goes away. It's written into the history of the city and will always be revisited.

Even though President Kennedy had made it clear that he was sympathetic to the civil rights cause, fortunately, the movement didn't stop after he was killed. There are certain events in the Civil Rights Movement that people think of when they look back on that time: mostly in Alabama and Mississippi. The truth is that the movement was taking place all over the south and everyone was aware of it. Of course, there was no name put on it then. Everyone was just living life, and responding to the injustice around us. All of the major national civil rights organizations of the time had offices in Dallas. The people of Dallas definitely played a role in the struggle.

One of the events that comes to mind when thinking about the movement in Dallas is the boycott of Piccadilly Cafeteria. Piccadilly was a big restaurant downtown at the time. There was a man named Clarence Broadnax who was actually the first black hairdresser to work at Neiman Marcus. He tried to go into Piccadilly to eat and was denied because he was black. That event sparked a boycott that lasted for almost a month. The boycott finally ended when the Civil Rights Act was signed in 1964 by President Lyndon B. Johnson, who took over for President Kennedy after his assassination.

The biggest event during the Civil Rights Movement in Dallas, in terms of the number of people, was the march that took place in 1965. The march was organized by the NAACP, and over 3,000 people marched in the downtown streets. What made this different was that a lot of the people who were marching were white, and they walked side by side with the black protesters. Even most of the white people downtown who didn't participate looked on and offered a tip of the cap or words of encouragement to the protesters. Of course, there were some who had something negative to say and tried to cause trouble, but they were so badly outnumbered that those incidents were kept to a minimum.

Again, when we were living through that time, we didn't look at it like it would be studied and talked about forever. Looking back on it, it makes me proud to see how the people of Dallas contributed to the Civil Rights Movement that made life better for people all around the country.

Around this time, I was making sure to go by and see Clara Jean a lot, because I was always concerned about her kids. I would go over as much as I could to see the children and make sure everything was ok.

"Clara Jean, are these kids in school?" I would ask.

"Girl, you need to mind your own business," she would say. It would be that type of conversation. Clara Jean had a lifestyle that she really enjoyed and she just enjoyed being free to party and do whatever she wanted. If someone didn't know us and came around, they would probably think that I was the older sister and she was the younger one based on how we interacted with each other.

"You don't have to raise my kids," she told me one day, because I was always on her. It always came from a place of love.

One day, Clara Jean was at the home of a girl named Jewel. From what I was told, the girl had some type of dispute with her husband. What started out as a dispute, turned into a fight, and that fight escalated to the point that Jewel pulled out a gun. Jewel began shooting at her husband, but Clara Jean was in the line of fire and got hit in her stomach. She was seven months pregnant at the time. The bullet hit her in the upper intestines. When I heard what happened, I couldn't get to the hospital soon enough. My heart was racing and my mind was racing even faster than that. *How could this happen? I can't lose her. Not now.*

It was devastating to lose my dad and mom for obvious reasons, but in both of those cases it happened gradually. It didn't make it any easier to accept, but I could make sense of it in my head. People get sick all the time. Sometimes people get really sick and they don't get well. This was something completely different. There was no sense to be made from this. I had known people who had gotten murdered, but this was my older sister: my family. She just couldn't die.

Once they treated her and got her stabilized, I was able to talk to her. She was heavily sedated but she was able to sit up and speak with me. After the fact, they believed that the medication that they gave her had settled in the baby's lungs. It caused her to go into labor. Now she had gone from worrying about trying to live, to trying to bring a baby into the world. The baby passed away during the delivery. After that, the doctors had to go through a lot to get Clara Jean stable again because the labor itself, and the emotions of losing the baby took a toll on her.

The next day, she seemed to be getting better but

there was some infection that they couldn't clear up. That became the problem that lingered day after day. They could never manage to clear up the infection. She was still conscious and aware of everything and she was able to talk like normal most of the time.

I would bring her three children up to the hospital to see her when I could. They wouldn't let little kids come in the hospital much back then. I would sneak them in to see her. She was up and alert.

She would say, "Well, I don't know if I'm going to make it. You take care of my kids."

"Uh-uh, you'll make it, I'm not raising no more kids," I laughed. I really thought she was going to be alright. I thought she had made it through the worst of it.

"I don't think I'ma make it," she said.

"Yeah, you gon' make it," I replied. "I'm not even thinking about that."

She was in the hospital for six weeks, two days and about three hours: I had it down. I know, because I was counting the moments until she could go home. Then, I received the devastating news that she had died. She was only 27 years old. I felt totally drained. I felt as if everything had just been sucked out of me.

I always thought that the worst thing that could happen was when I lost my mother, but the loss of my oldest sister was just a different type of loss. It brought an entirely different feeling. She used to always take up for me, and she wouldn't let anybody bother me. She was everything to me and she was killed. I'll never forget how it was all over the news back then, on television and in the newspaper. It became a big story for whatever reason.

I think the girl went to jail behind the incident. After a while, I just wanted it behind me so I didn't follow up. I didn't really care. There was nothing that they could do to that girl that would bring my big sister back. I couldn't really muster up the energy to care at that point. They called me on a couple occasions and I had to go to court about it. The girl called me a couple times to explain what happened and to apologize. I told her I wasn't really interested in discussing it, but I also let her know that I didn't have any bitterness in my heart.

Clara Jean left behind three children: Ronnie, Verneana, and Artemis. Artemis' father got custody of him. Ronnie and Verneana came to live with us. There wasn't really a lot of thought involved in it. Just like I knew I had to take care of my brothers and sisters, I knew I had to take care of my sister's children. It was just that simple for me. At that point, I just put it in the Lord's hands and I put my focus on raising the kids so they could have their lives affected as little as possible by what had happened to their mom.

5 FAMILY TIES

Ms. Price zips down the highway, darting in and out of traffic, headed towards Cowboys' stadium on the morning of the game. When Ms. Price is driving, headed for a game, items and passengers tend to tumble around in the car, similar to an amusement park ride.

"You remember that song that said, 'would you like to swing on our star? Uh-huh.' You remember that? Let's go, let's go sir!" she says to the back of a car blocking her in the fast lane. "We've got a game sir."

"You alright Ms. Earline?"

"Uh huh, I'm wonderful."

"I thought you were going to grab a hat to wear." Ms. Price is accessorized in Dallas Cowboys apparel from head to toe, as usual on the day of a game, and apparently wants to make sure that her guests are as well. "There's a sun visor back there." "You know what I'll do? I think I'm going to wear just this black and white hat and get a star to put up there."

"Oh, naw, not in Cowboys Stadium darling. There's

a visor back there."

"You don't want me to just wear this?" Earline holds up a black and white striped hat.

"Are you crazy? Zebra stripes with a Cowboys' star? Is there something wrong with you? Zebra stripes in Cowboys' country?" Ms. Price has a way of asking someone if they're crazy, or if something is wrong with them in the least harmless way possible. It's not an actual question, but more like the most humorous, rhetorical one imaginable. Usually, the person on the receiving end of the question can't do anything but laugh, because it forces them to think back on whatever they just said or did to cause her to ask the question, and everyone around gets a good laugh out of it.

"Alright, I'll use the visor," Earline relents with a chuckle.

"Well you don't have to, but it's back there."

"No, I will. I wanted something on my head."

"I always try to keep something in my car just in case...you never know," Ms. Price explains. For her, she means she never knows when, like a super hero with an alter ego, she'll need to change from Ms. Price the loving mother, grandmother and all-around great family member and office manager, into Ms. Price the Cowboys' #1 Fan, loved and revered by virtually every Cowboys' fan she encounters.

In the late 70's, I began attending every single Cowboys home game. It was no longer just a matter of going when I was able, unless I was too sick to move, I was going to be there. That wasn't always the case.

One day Charmayne said, "Mama you don't know this, but really you invented tailgating." I just laughed. I didn't think of it like that, but I just knew I wanted to be at the games, even if we couldn't go in. For the whole family to attend the games would have been really expensive, so sometimes instead of watching on television, I would go down with Willie and all of the kids and we would park outside of the stadium. We would pack lunches with sandwiches, potato chips and something to drink and we would listen to the game outside of the stadium on the big loudspeakers. It was so much fun. After it was over and they had won or lost, we would just head on back down the road.

Around this time though, I was able to start getting tickets to all of the games, and that's when I really began to meet a lot of the Cowboys' players in person. There was Randy White, Roger Staubach, and Tony Dorsett: I met a lot of them. Randy White came to the team in 1975. He was a backup for the first couple of years and then he just broke out and became one of the most important players on the team. He was a player who was always really polite to the fans.

Of course, Roger Staubach is one of the most famous Cowboys of them all, and for good reason. Roger was also a backup for the first couple of years on the team and he paid his dues like everyone else, even though he was a star player in college. He actually went and fulfilled his four-year commitment to the Navy after he was drafted before he came to the Cowboys, and that impressed a lot of people. The very first year that he took over as the starting quarterback was the first year that we won the Super Bowl. It was great! It wasn't even close. We beat the Miami Dolphins 24-3 and Roger was the MVP. I tell you, we celebrated after that one.

The first person to ever sign my jersey for me was Rayfield Wright. He went to the Hall of Fame a few years ago. Rayfield was the one who used to protect Roger Staubach. They came to the team around the same time. Roger always said he was the best. He always unselfishly gave him a lot of credit for his own success. He was known for having really quick feet for being such a big man.

When I met him, he said, "I don't know a lot of things, and I ain't been a lot of places, but one thing I know, is I'm a Dallas Cowboy."

I said, "Go on then Rayfield!" Because that sounded beautiful to me. I remember that day I had on my leather hat that I used to wear. I would go down on the field and get their gloves and souvenirs after the game. One day, I was out shopping and ran into Rayfield Wright's wife some years after he had retired.

I told her, "I miss y'all!" We exchanged hugs and she let me know what Rayfield and the rest of their family was up to. The players' families are like my family so I miss them all when I don't see them. Generally, I run into them from time to time and we get to catch up on what's going on. They can never know how much of a relief they were for me, at times, when I could just come to the game and forget about any negative aspects of my life that I might have been facing. For that three hours, and the time after the game amongst the players, there was no abuse, no sickness and no death. It was like they were doing me a favor that they didn't understand. There were a lot of times when I needed to be distracted from life. For that period of time, at least, it seems like my problems went away.

Randy White gave me a picture and signed it and that was like getting a jersey for me at that time. I cherished that and I still have it. Danny White was really nice, and Craig Morton was too. I can remember standing places and just interacting with them and just feeling so happy because I was always a huge fan. They were very approachable and they let us know they were just people like anybody else. It didn't start with the TV cameras or anything like that. I remember one day I saw Willie Townsend, who was a good player for us back in the 70's, and he called over to me.

"Hey," he said. "How you doing young lady?" At that time, I was almost as young as they were.

"Ms. Price, you're not built bad at all," he said.

"Are you married?"

"Yes," I said, just as I always would. Now, I

cannot sit here and say that I know he wanted to date me. Some of them would say things, or pay a compliment, "Ms. Price, you're nice looking," but nobody said, "Hey, where do you live?" or "what's your phone number?" It was never that type of interaction. They knew I was there because I really loved the game. There were enough other women there who didn't and were there just with hopes of getting with one of them. They knew the difference. Sometimes when they'd lose, I would just sit there and cry long after the game was over. I was there for the game, and I always loved the game.

I remember it really hurt me when Roger Staubach retired. I can picture standing right in front of the same TV that's sitting in my living room today and watching him on the screen when he said, "Today will be the last time I step on the field for The Cowboys."

"Oh my God!" I yelled. It was a real loss. It was like having a relative tell you they're moving away and you won't be seeing them anymore.

I got into banking, and worked in that field off and on for about seventeen years. I didn't work when I first got married. I started working different part-time jobs to help out and that ended up leading to a career in banking. It wasn't my intention at the time. At that point, I was just doing what I could to help out. I worked as a babysitter for some people and did other odd jobs here and there occasionally.

I worked for LTV for a while, which is an

aerospace company. Later on, they changed the name to Vought. The company manufactured airplanes and missiles and all kinds of weapons. I worked in accounting. We pulled orders, and when the buyers would get parts for the planes, we would have to set up all the paperwork so they could order them and get paid for it. This is around the time when things really began to switch over to computers. We were using computers and they were just really becoming popular then. This was the late 70's, and even though things had changed from when we were young, the reality was that there were still not that many black people working at most of the large companies in Dallas. So, there weren't that many black people out there where I was. On the huge floor where we worked, there was probably only about 5 or 6 of us.

After the tragedies that I had endured, and other unfortunate situations that I found myself in, things began to get more and more complicated in my life with my husband. Verneana and Ronnie had become a permanent part of my household, and I just wanted us to live the life we were supposed to be living: raising the children together as a family. I didn't want to marry into someone's family but not be a part of their family. What's the point of that? I became completely uncomfortable around them as a direct result of things that I would hear them say.

When I would take the kids by his mom's house, she would say things like, "Oh, that's her dead sister's kids there." What kind of way is that to address somebody? You're just going to talk about my sister in the way? You'll speak to children like that? They were very insensitive in that situation, and I couldn't understand that. If you have a problem with me, that's one thing. I didn't understand how you could refuse to embrace children who had gone through what they had been through when we were supposed to be family. Through it all, I was still me, so even though they made me feel that way, I didn't give them the satisfaction of knowing it. They knew not to play with me directly, but they were disrespectful enough to make their feelings clear. They knew how far they could push without me letting them have it.

The way that certain members of his family behaved towards me was one thing, but sometimes you're forced to take on the burdens of members of that same family, just because an unexpected situation might come up. When you have a good heart, you'll often find yourself doing this even when certain people haven't treated you well. Of course, I knew all about that. That was the story of my life. It's what I was raised to do.

He had a sister who struggled with alcohol, and I had to help with her kids. Besides that, his grandfather, Willie Lee Price, lived here in town, but he had been abandoned by pretty much everyone else, and was in horrible shape. He had to have surgery.

We stepped in and we were there to help him. We had a lot of issues going on taking care of our families. It was alright because I had been raised well and I knew how to cook, pay bills, manage the household, and all of the other things that I needed to be doing. That's what kept things pretty stable. I was the backbone of my family. Most of the girls around me in my generation had their mothers and grandmothers to help them out, but I didn't have that. So, I had no choice but to go forward. But with all of those things going on, at some point, you're going to have cracks in the foundation that you build.

One day, after what seemed like forever, I received the wonderful news that I had received custody of my brothers and sisters and they were able to come home to me. Of course, the woman fought it to the end, and was mad because she wasn't going to get the check anymore. The nerve of some people. We had overcome a lot of obstacles despite the fact that we had lost our mother and father far too soon. We lost them at a time when our futures hadn't even been close to decided yet, and we really needed guidance and help with our lives. But despite all of that, every single one of us graduated from high school. I was so proud of all of them.

When my baby brother graduated, the diploma was mailed to Hazel's house because they still had her address. Would you believe that this woman destroyed the thing out of spite? When he got it, it was all balled up, and I had to take him to a printing shop and have it recreated. Buck and Phyllis came back to live with me, and our household grew much larger. My sister Florence got married to a man named Leonard who she had been dating, so she didn't come back.

We were looking for a house to move into and I found a house in South Dallas. I called the lady who owned it. It turned out that her daughter went to school with my brother, and her son knew me.

"It's just me, my husband and my baby," I told her. I didn't necessarily think it was best to mention everyone. Later on she said, "I went over there and saw all these kids and I wanted to say something to you, but my house has never been this well-kept, including the yard and everything." I made sure that we took great care of the property and that the rent was always paid on time.

My younger brother Buck started a controversy in the family with a particular dating choice he'd made. What ended up happening was complicated. Buck started dating a girl whose cousin was a girl who my sister's husband was cheating on my sister with, if that makes any sense. So, my brother-in-law would take Buck with him on weekends and they would basically double date with the mistress and her cousin.

Buck messed around and married this girl, and that ended up causing a big rift in the family. As far as everyone was concerned, he was sleeping with the enemy and had basically co-signed the infidelity of my sister's husband. It was as if he had chosen the friendship of his brother-in-law over loyalty to his sister. I was really disappointed, but it was the choice he made.

Around this time, Charmayne became good friends with Karis, who became my goddaughter. They were in high school together. Of course, she didn't start out as my goddaughter. I have a way of bringing genuine people into my family, and before I know it, they seem as if they were always there.

They both graduated a year early from high school. The following year, their bond and friendship went to another level and Karis was around a lot more. At that time, she began staying at our house on weekends because her father's job would send him to St. Louis for work, and her mother would go with him. So she wouldn't have to be at home alone, Karis began staying over at our house regularly.

This was during the disco era, and Charmayne, Karis and my nephew Ronnie began to hang out and go out to clubs together. I was always sitting there waiting up for them to make sure that they made it in safely. When they arrived, I would just sit up and talk with them and they would tell me all about their night and funny things that had happened.

I got a kick out of their little experiences as they were growing up. I didn't really get to have those times because I had to grow up so fast. This was a different era, and it was before crack was in the streets, so it was safer than what it would become later. Of course, there were still negative things out there to get into, but nothing like what the crack era would bring later.

I had a dark green deuce and a quarter, which is what people called a Buick Electra, and sometimes I would let them take my car when they went out. Karis had a pale yellow, Plymouth Barracuda, and they always talked about how embarrassed they were to be seen in it. They called it "The Bear." At times when I didn't let them use my car, they would park about three blocks away from the club and walk up to the club so no one would see them. Charmayne had a Monte Carlo at the time.

Verneana had gotten married, but to be honest, her husband was a bum and he was very abusive. I really hated that for her because she thought she had a great guy. That's usually how it seems at first. He was a really handsome fellow and he was polite, but he was a bum. Behind closed doors, she was exposed to another side of him. So, she took her two kids and left and was staying in some apartments in the Cedar Crest area of town.

I figured this was a chance for her, and that she might be able to make it. I just put it in God's hands and prayed for the best. I always wanted to protect my kids and take care of all of them, but you can't do that forever. She had two children, and I used to go get the kids from her on weekends to try to help her out and make the load as light as possible for her.

Charmayne and Karis enrolled at Mountain View College together, so they would go to class and then go back to my house and raid my refrigerator, frying up all of my potatoes and watching soap operas. Then, around three o'clock, there would be a mad dash to clean up the house and have it back in order by the time I arrived from work. Of course, I didn't find out about them frying up all of my potatoes until later.

My nephew Ronnie was really just a sweetheart. He didn't grow to be a big guy. He was about medium height, with dark skin and had really pretty teeth. Unfortunately for Ronnie, the Jheri curl era had just begun, and he didn't have quite enough hair for a curl. Everybody else was getting curls, but he just couldn't grow his hair out enough. The girls would try to improvise and use a relaxer to get a similar look.

There was a commercial on at the time that would sing, "Goodbye Mr. Francis, I can perm my hair all by myself...," and they would just sing that jingle and crack up laughing. That was the funniest thing to them. He was a good sport about it though. The results were hit or miss, and he would end up being the butt of a running joke by the girls. He went to work every day, and he was so nice that after working all week long, he would be Charmayne and Karis' babysitter so they could go out if they wanted to. On top of that, he would give them money to go out. He loved to dance and was a sweet-natured, outgoing, charismatic guy. He also went to school with Charmayne and Karis.

Ronnie was more like my child than my nephew because he was only three years old when Clara Jean was killed. I was the only mother he had known, so he was really close to me. He was as close to me as Charmayne was. They were born the same year and they had the bond of a brother and sister.

Charmayne had been dating a guy named Leonard for a while by that point and they eventually got married. She gave birth to a beloved baby girl, Chloe. The marriage didn't last long. Unfortunately, she got married at a time when she wasn't mature enough to handle it. After Charmayne got married, Ronnie moved with her and lived with her and her husband for a while.

One night, while I was in bed, I was awakened by a phone call. What the person on the other end of the line told me shook me to my core. Because I had been sleeping, I wondered whether I was dreaming or not: my niece Verneana had been stabbed, rushed to the hospital and was in critical condition. Lord, how could this be happening? You hear people talk about cycles, and generational curses, but I never really give much credit to the thought. But here we were, years after Clara Jean was murdered, and her daughter that I had taken in and raised was fighting for her life. I felt helpless. I felt like she had needed me and I had not been able to save her.

A girl named Toni stabbed her during some type of altercation, and they just let her lay there until she bled to death. Supposedly, she interfered in someone's business somehow and the girl stabbed her is all I was told. She never smoked, never got drunk, and never did drugs, but she was hanging around company that put her in that type of environment. I didn't even know who the girl was who was on the phone telling me this.

I just told her, "bring my babies to the hospital," because I didn't want to take a chance trying to go pick the kids up myself and getting to Neana too late.

When I got to Parkland, someone from the hospital greeted me and asked, "Are you the mother?"

"Yes, I am…well, I'm the auntie actually," I explained. "I raised them." They told me that she had lost too much blood, and for me to come with them. The doctor told me that if they would have called the ambulance when it first happened, they probably would have been able to save her. Instead, everybody got scared, left and let her lay there and bleed until it was too late.

These two guys were on either side of me as we walked and it looked like we were in the longest hallway I had ever seen. They brought me to where she was and she was hooked up to a ventilator with tubes in her mouth. They couldn't save her. I started sobbing. I was devastated.

A while later, her husband showed up and claimed her body. He was supposedly going to get some people to give him some money to bury her because he didn't have any insurance. I knew a few different people who owned funeral homes here in Dallas: one was Walter Wilson in Cedar Crest. Neana had laid up there and gotten to the point where she had started swelling and this boy still didn't have the money to bury her. He's thinking that we're taking up money from people and then we were going to give it to him to bury her. When I realized what he was doing, I went straight to Walter.

He asked, "Carolyn, do you want me to bury her?"

"Yes, but not on his behalf," I told him. "We'll handle it." So, we finally got her buried.

That's how I ended up taking in De'Leacia, Verneana's daughter, to raise her. We call her Dee for short. I went and got her and brought her home with me. She had just turned three years old, and she was always around me anyway, so it wasn't a drastic change to where she had to get to know me or anything like that. At that point, Charmayne couldn't really raise her baby and give her the care that she needed. She was dealing with her own issues and I just didn't feel that she was mature enough to give her the care that she needed so I decided to step in. That's when I took in Chloe, Charmayne's daughter. After my brothers and sisters, and Charmayne and Clara Jean's kids, I now had a third generation of family members to raise.

Shortly after that, Ronnie reunited with his

father and moved in with him. Ronnie was bouncing around by that time, and I think he was just really trying to find who he was, to see what he needed to do in the world. The neighborhood that he moved to was really bad and there were a lot of drugs around, and of course, that brings a lot of violence.

I believe he just got caught up in a world that was way over his head. Twenty-one can be a really great or terrible age depending on where your mind is. If you have a sense of purpose and you know where you're going in life, it's great, because you feel invincible. But if you're just drifting, have no idea where you're going, and you're surrounded by negative influences, it can be a recipe for disaster.

I have no idea why Ronnie was sleeping in an abandoned apartment. They say that's where he was. I don't know if he and his father had a problem or some kind of falling out, but he was sleeping in an abandoned apartment in the same complex where he lived with his father.

I do not know the circumstances that led up to the act, but I know that someone shot him to death in that apartment. That was just a tremendous period of sadness. You just look at someone who was such a sweet person and they just end up lost. How many more times could we be devastated as a family? How many more times would we have our hearts broken? My life with Willie didn't get better, it got worse. Truthfully, he was a man that just had an evil spirit in him for some reason. He was always doing things, and there were signs that I should have seen, or actually did see, but I was the type of person who was always trying to make sure that everything was ok. I would justify things and sweep them under the rug. Maybe it's not so bad. Maybe it's just his friends he's around. That's how I felt.

A lot of the problems came from people around him and it was just jealousy and stupidity. Willie's sister used to call me and tell me that my mother-in-law would have women at church with Willie. He didn't go to church with me, but all of a sudden he was attending his mother's church because the girl he was courting was at that church. All the while, his mother stood by and supported it. It got very hard. Then I found out that he had been going with the lady for years at that point. It was very disrespectful to me, among other things.

I went through a lot with him. I was cussed out, jumped on, everything. He also became physically abusive. He was the type that would cheat, and then lash out at me because he got caught. If I found out he was courting somebody else or doing something that he didn't have any business doing, that's usually when he would get physical with me. He would get mad and push me around. He didn't go as far as just holding me down and beating me to the point of giving me black eyes and things like that. He would do things like hold me down, twist my arms, or choke me.

At times like that I would always go back to

the fact that I didn't have my parents. Despite what some people think, you still need your parents when you get grown. It doesn't automatically change because you become an adult. I needed someone in my corner to stand up for me, or at least stand with me, and I didn't have it. That person would have been Clara Jean, but I didn't have her anymore either.

His family always thought that if he wasn't with me, then I wouldn't be successful. They thought I was dependent on him to the point where I was using him, but that was far from the truth, and they found that out later. He was a provider, a really great one, but they found out who was really the backbone of the household. Everything I have, by the grace of God, I did by myself: no husband, nothing. I did this with the help of the Lord.

I always gave people the benefit of the doubt when I could, and overall, definitely more than people deserved. I underestimated a lot of people and just did not think people were capable of some of the underhanded things that they did. I thought the way that I treated people was common. I thought it was just the way that you were supposed to live. I was always trying to help someone else out and do things for other people. I didn't know that people could be so envious. I guess I was naïve for that, but that's how I saw it. I didn't think people wanted what you had so badly that they would stoop to unthinkable acts to get it. I didn't think of it like that. His family figured that if they could get Willie away from me, then I would lose, and they would have his support again.

Even though my husband was abusive, which should have been enough to walk away, what eventually brought the marriage to an end was the women. He was just constantly messing with other women and there's no way to have peace of mind when the person who's supposed to love you is living that type of lifestyle. He eventually ended up with the woman that I had been told was attending church with him and his mother. They claimed this woman was doing witchcraft or something crazy like that, and had done something to him. I don't know what she did because I didn't let her bother me. The bottom line is that the choices he made created the consequences that we both dealt with. That woman wouldn't have been able to do anything that the door wasn't opened for her to do.

Things had broken apart so much that when he finally went for the divorce, I simply said, "Go for it." What else was there to say? By that time, it was long overdue. The natural reaction is to be hurt, and I was certainly pretty hurt at first. Even in those kind of situations where a person is clearly in the wrong, there is still a disheartening feeling that comes along with being a part of a failed marriage.

*With our owner Jerry Jones (top) and legendary
quarterback Roger Staubach (bottom)*

*With Hall of Fame players running back Emmitt Smith (top)
and quarterback Troy Aikman (bottom)*

With my favorite Dallas Cowboy of them all, "The Playmaker" Michael Irvin

*With NBA superstar LeBron James (top) and one of the
greatest R&B groups of all time
Boyz II Men (bottom)*

With our former coach Bill Parcells (top) and our current coach Jason Garrett (bottom)

*With our quarterback Tony Romo (top) and wide receiver
Dez Bryant (bottom)*

With our newest young stars Dak Prescott (top) and Ezekiel Elliott (bottom)

With Hall of Fame wide receiver Drew Pearson, the great Ed "Too Tall Jones and former linebacker Eugene "The Hit Machine" Lockhart (top) and Chloe with the original Cowboys' superfan "Crazy Ray" (bottom)

*With our former All-Pro linebacker Demarcus Ware (top)
and former All-Pro safety Darren Woodson (bottom)*

*With our tight end Jason Witten (top) and former
quarterback Quincy Carter (bottom)*

*With our Hall of Fame Defensive Tackle Bob Lilly (top) and
our Executive Vice President Stephen Jones (bottom)*

With our Hall of Fame running back Tony Dorsett (top) and with
Charlotte Jones-Anderson and Gene Jones (bottom)

With former wide receiver Joey Galloway (top) and
filmmaker Tyler Perry (bottom)

*Enjoying training camp with my girls Charmayne, Chloe,
Charde and Dee (top) and me and my younger sisters (l to
r) Carolyn Mopping-Price Sandra Mopping Johnson,
Florence Mopping-Rollins and Phyllis Mopping-Jones
(bottom)*

With reporter Yulonda Hadnot of KTEV-TV in Texarkana and NFL official Ed Hochuli (top) Hall of Fame boxer Oscar De la Hoya (below)

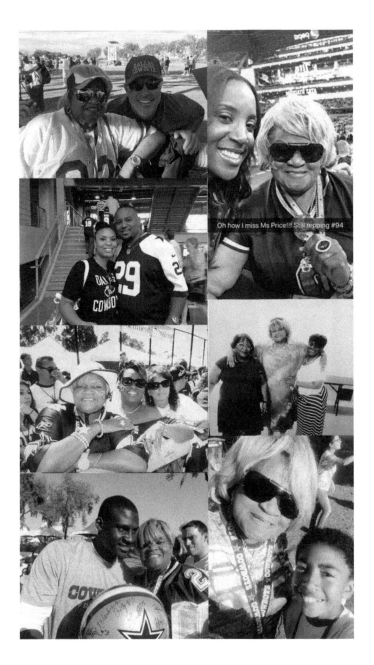

Oh how I miss Ms Price!!! Still repping #94

6 PROS AND CONS

Approaching the stadium, Ms. Price turns into a tour guide, always concerned with making sure that anyone who is with her has everything they need to enjoy themselves.

"Ok, so I have two big tailgates out here if y'all want to eat--" *her thoughts are interrupted by a beep from her car indicating that it is low on gas.* "Are you kidding me? I didn't check my gas. I have not checked my gas and it just came on. I know one thing, we're close to the stadium now. I thinking about my Cowboys that much that I didn't notice my gas hand."

As she pulls into a gas station near the stadium, she reaches into the backseat to retrieve her purse. "Look in my purse and get my credit card please."

Moments later, Earline produces a credit card and hands it to her. Of course, it's a Dallas Cowboys credit card. "Check that out, *she holds it out.* People say their fans of their teams, I bet they don't have a credit card with their team on it, ha!"

"Is your tank on this side?" *Earline, apparently*

wanting to help out by pumping the gas for her, seeks clarification. As always, Ms. Price's sharp wit is on full display, even in the most seemingly inconsequential situations.

"You think a woman my age, that's been driving this car since it rolled out of General Motors, would park on the wrong side of the gas pump? Are you kidding me?" She immediately jumps out of the car refusing any assistance with pumping the gas. She'll do it.

As she finishes pumping the gas, she is recognized by a Detroit Lions fan who's in town for the game. The woman obviously recognizes Ms. Price and seizes the opportunity to shoot a little trash talk her way.

"Whooo! Ms. Cowboy, your Cowboys in trouble today. I don't think they know what they're in for. They ain't ready for Detroit!" The excited fan shouts at Ms. Price. From inside the car, Cynthia looks on and is well aware of what's coming next.

"Uh-oh," Cynthia utters.

"We from Detroit!"

Ms. Price calmly gazes at the Lions fan and replies, "I can tell by looking at your car. Talkin' about she from Detroit. We can tell!" The woman and her significant other are standing next to an older model, grey SUV with some years of wear and rust on it. The plain, grey older SUV stands in stark contrast to Ms. Price's shiny new Cadillac, decorated with Dallas Cowboys' stars on the side and flags on the mirror. "DON'T START WITH ME!" Ms. Price grows louder and other fans in the gas station parking lot erupt into laughter. As usual, the targets of Ms. Price's sharp retort can't do much more than stand and chuckle.

Ms. Price then takes aim at her shirt. "Where's your lion at girl? WHERE'S YOUR LION AT! Get yourself TOGETHER! American Eagle? Where your lion?" More people in the vicinity hear the exchange and gather around and enjoy the impromptu roasting session. "You say you a lion, I didn't even know y'all were still in the NFL! What is wrong with you?" It's all laughter and big smiles around the gas pumps now as Ms. Price is in rare form, speaking loudly enough to be heard all the way to the street.

"Take a picture with me right here," the fan concedes defeat in the friendly trash talking session and requests a picture with Ms. Price.

"Y'all drive all the way down here baby?" Ms. Price asks, now switching back to her motherly tone.

"Yeah, but not from Detroit. We stay in Oklahoma now," she explains.

"Oh ok, baby," Ms. Price notices the attire of her boyfriend. "And get those pants up baby. Get those pants up. Look like a young man. That ain't cute." The young man smiles sheepishly after being lectured about his sagging pants in the middle of a gas station parking lot by a woman he's never met, but he pulls them up.

"Thank you. Take care of yourself baby, y'all enjoy the game," Ms. Price enters her vehicle before being held up by one last question from the fan.

"Where's the best place to park? Give us some good tips," says the Lions fan.

"Well, I don't know, we're high class here so they take care of us," Ms. Price replies and can't resist getting in one final dig in on the way out for her audience. "Look how that

car look, talkin' about she from Detroit, CAN'T YOU TELL BY LOOKIN' AT 'EM?" Ms. Price is now laughing as loudly as everyone else in between words. "I was minding my own business pulling up to get some gas, she talking about 'I'm from Detroit,' I CAN TELL!" There's now an even bigger chorus of laughter and actual applause from people standing around. The male Detroit fan now actually grabs his girlfriend by the arm.

"Don't say another word," he says smiling.

"You betta get away from me," Ms. Price warns.

"You'd better get out of here," another Cowboys' fan who's been watching nearby chimes in. "That's the biggest Cowboys' fan there is!" He adds.

"Talk to 'em, talk to 'em," Ms. Price playfully advises. "Y'all have a good one baby, enjoy the game," Ms. Price adds as she gets into her car.

"Ok, you too ma'am," the Lions fan replies. Like countless other people, she now has her own personal Ms. Price encounter that she'll never forget.

By 1990, I had been working in banking for about seventeen years. I loved it. Anyone who knows me knows that I'm a people person. Working in a bank was great because I had a chance to talk to people every day from all different walks of life. I had a chance to help people, even if sometimes if was in a small way. At this time, I was working for NCNB Bank in the Oak Cliff section of Dallas. I had a great relationship with my customers, and I was known for that. Just as much as people would come to know me later for my association with the Cowboys, I was already known that much in the community just for being myself and the way that I dealt with people. I treated every customer with respect, and I was professional. Some of my customers were Cowboys players.

One day, a man named Fritz McMillon walked into the bank. He came in with Bobby Silmon, who owned a well-known auto repair shop in Oak Cliff. Bobby was a frequent customer of ours, so when he recommended Fritz and said he would be a good customer, his recommendation meant something.

I had never come across him before, but it wouldn't have been unusual if I had. Up until that point, I had done a lot of work in the community and I had dealt with so many customers that I was exposed to a variety of people. Recently, they had opened up a mini-bank on the lower level of the bank and made me supervisor over that branch, so I was given more responsibility.

On the surface, Fritz was a charming, articulate, successful businessman. He said that he owned car dealerships in several states. He came in dressed in expensive clothes, talked the talk, and if there's such a thing as looking like a millionaire, then he would fit that description. It wasn't just me that was impressed. He mingled with most of the employees in the bank, not just tellers, but loan officers and others. He was a really charismatic person, so no one really suspected him of being anything but who he appeared to be.

The truth of the matter is that he was a con artist who had perpetrated fraud in several states across the country, and had already served time in federal prison for his crimes. If I had known that, of course, things would have gone a completely different way. Later on, I found out a lot that I wish I had known earlier.

In The *Dallas Morning News*, they went into details about him and his cons. One common scheme he pulled was to become friends with three different customers of one of his car lots and convince them all to pay him in advance to purchase the same expensive luxury car at a discount. He would then give one customer the car, another customer the title, and the other customer nothing before leaving town with all of their money. Sometimes he played the role of a minister. He could play the organ and sing like a professional so he was convincing.

There wasn't much he had done that was a secret to law enforcement. According to the FBI, Fritz had changed his appearance a number of times to successfully pull of his cons. He had also used over 30 alias names since the 1960's. He had run scams in Denver, Colorado, Atlanta, Georgia, Toledo, Ohio, Baton Rouge and Shreveport, Louisiana, and Gulfport, Mississippi. Those were the ones they knew about.

When it came to banks, his schemes were what they called kiting checks. What he would do is open a new account at two different banks. Then, he would write checks on one account and cash them at the other, but there wouldn't be enough money in the accounts to cover the checks. He was great at the main part of the con: making the teller comfortable enough not to check and see if the funds were available at the other bank. That was my mistake. He would do enough legitimate business with the bank, so that by the time the con came, you had relaxed because he was such a good customer. He had been sent to prison for pulling the same con at another bank in Dallas. When he got out, our bank was his next target.

For the first couple of months that he was a customer, he was a good one. He made regular deposits, many of them large, and we didn't have any problems. All through August, and into September of that year, he was a regular customer, and a good one. One day, in September, he bought twenty cashier's checks totaling more than five hundred-thousand dollars. The amount of money wasn't shocking. We had many customers with a lot of money who came in the bank and conducted transactions for large amounts of money. It was nothing new. It was business as usual at the bank. As bank employees, we were told to use our best judgement when it came to a customer.

By that point, Fritz had established himself as

a trusted customer. It wasn't like it is now at a bank, where everything was on the screen right in front you, in real time, when someone deposited or withdrew money. There was a process to verify the money, and I didn't do it. I gave him the same benefit of the doubt that I had given other customers many times before. That was my mistake, and I wasn't the only one to make it. Besides our bank, he pulled the same con at First Interstate Bank of Texas-Oak Cliff, along with several other schemes he had pulled on residents in Dallas. That's why I wasn't worried about it at first. I thought that they would just reprimand me, or at the very worst, terminate me. That was my biggest worry: losing my job. Never in my wildest dreams did I think it would go any further than that.

I cooperated with them, turned over everything they asked for, and told them everything I knew, but yet I still woke up early in the morning, in my own home, with FBI agents pointing guns in my face, yelling at me, telling me not to move.

At that point, I was just afraid. Once they put the guns away and the reality set in, I was shocked, and devastated. I didn't understand how it made sense for me to be under arrest. This was a man who had a documented history of this behavior going back over twenty years in many different cities and states across the nation. He had used aliases and disguises, successfully stolen millions of dollars, and had gone to prison for it.

While he was doing all of that all across the

country, I was in one city: Dallas. I was in the same city that I was born and raised in. I was in the same city where I'd had to grow up far too soon and be responsible for the well-being of so many other people. I was working at a place where I loved my customers and they loved me. I had built relationships with so many people in the community. I had volunteered and worked on the campaigns of prominent politicians in the city for years. I was very active in the community. I had endured so much tragedy and I was still standing.

Why would I throw all of that away: my career, my family, and possibly my natural life, to all of a sudden be the accomplice of a career criminal in a bank scheme? That's a question that a lot of people in the community wanted answered. The prosecutor on the case didn't understand where all of the support that I received was coming from.

"Why is she so popular?" the prosecutor asked my attorney.

"Why don't you go over there and ask her," he replied.

In court, they never presented any evidence that I received any money from him. They didn't even argue that I had. They didn't try to argue that I did it for any romantic reasons, which is the other thing you'd think they would suggest. They couldn't say that either because I didn't ever deal with him outside of the bank, and he never put his hands on me. I always kept the relationship professional. So again, why would I risk throwing my entire life away in a situation like this? It didn't add up, and I wasn't the only person who could see that.

They charged me with conspiracy to commit fraud and aiding and abetting. It was like one long, bad dream. A tremendous amount of people from all over the city stood up for me: they showed up and showed out. They were outraged. People rallied around me so much that I was overwhelmed. Pettis Norman, an ex-Cowboy player, testified during my trial. Other players spoke up on my behalf also. I knew that I was popular in the city and that I had a lot of friends, but that doesn't always guarantee anything. A person can be popular when they're up and everyone can run away when the bad times come, but that didn't happen to me.

The support came from so many different people in the community, and throughout Dallas as a whole. There were ministers, community leaders, politicians, customers, Cowboys players: so many people stepped up to defend me and speak on my behalf. I tell you another thing: it wasn't just black people. There were white people along with the black people supporting me and fighting to keep me free. Even the U.S. attorney who was prosecuting the case said that the reason I was the only one being tried was because they couldn't find Fritz. I believe that not only was that the reason why I was the only one being tried, I also believe it was the only reason I was being tried at all. He had gone on the run, and they couldn't find him. If they had caught him as soon as a warrant went out for his arrest, I really think they would have left me alone. But since he took off, and they had no idea where to find him, somebody had to pay.

Knowing all of this made me nervous, but I was still confident. I guess I was naïve to believe it, but I really thought that the facts should make it an easy decision in my favor. When I arrived to the hearing where there were sentencing me, the officer at the door didn't recognize me and tried to turn me around.

"If you're going to the Price hearing, there are no more seats," he said.

"Well, let me turn around and go back then, even though I am Ms. Price," I said jokingly.

"Oh no, come on in then, we have a seat for you," he smiled. That's how crowded it was with people supporting me. We went in and took our seats. My heart felt like it was beating hard enough to see through my shirt, but I was still confident. To me, it was simple. This man was a career criminal who had a long track record of pulling acts like this, and leaving victims behind after the damage was done. I was one of those victims. I didn't even understand why you would attempt to prosecute a victim, which is what I was. I made the front page of the paper with a picture from that hearing, and Karis was in the picture with me.

I had taken care of my family my whole life

when they needed me: first, my siblings, then Clara Jean's children, and at this point, Neana's children, and of course, Chloe. My reputation meant everything to me. My word meant everything to me. When customers came into that bank, they knew who they were dealing with, and they loved me because of it. I developed so many relationships with good people. There were people who I was able to help out and there were people who had helped me out in situations. You could've interviewed all of them, every single one of them, and none of them would have had a negative word to say about my character. That was precious. That was something that you can't just manufacture, or buy with money. That is something you earn over time. *Time.*

Ultimately, after all the talking was done, the judge said, "we sentence you to 33 ½ months."

It was like I had been hit with a sledgehammer. I couldn't believe it. I wasn't the only person in the courtroom with tears coming down my face. The courtroom was full, and there were a lot of people crying along with me.

"I'm going to fight this with everything I've got," I told them on my way out. I said that and I meant it. It was what I had been doing my whole life. When an obstacle came in my path, I fought. It was all I knew to do.

After they convicted me, the support from everyone seemed like it increased even more. Dr. Willie Harris, one of our customers, and a well-known businessman, put fliers together and handed them out around the city to bring attention to my case. He told anyone who would listen that my attorney mishandled my case and that the bank treated me unfairly when they let me go. People questioned why the employees who opened his account or who were responsible for overseeing my work were not fired or arrested. These were valid questions to ask.

There were procedures in place, and even though I made a mistake in the process by not verifying the funds on certain transactions, there was a part of the process that was over my head. No bank employee could conduct transactions for that amount of money and be the only person with their eyes on the transactions. I was made to be a scapegoat, and a lot of people were extremely upset about it.

Rev. Wayne Mitchell, who was then the associate pastor at Oak Cliff Bible Fellowship, was one of a group of ministers and church members throughout the city who wrote letters to the judge. They pleaded with the judge to sentence me to community service that could be completed in an alternative program that the church ran. Darren Reagan, president of the Black State Employees Association of Texas also came out and spoke on my behalf. It provided a measure of comfort to my heart to see such overwhelming support coming from so many people, even after the conviction. It wasn't until later that year, in September, that they finally caught up to Fritz. They found him in a small

Mississippi town called Wiggins. He had been on the run for nearly a year.

Even in such a trying time, God was so good to me and there are a lot of news articles to prove it. It was because he was so good to me that the situation turned out the way it did, because it could have been much worse. It was the media coverage shining a light on the situation that ultimately paved the way for my freedom. When all the articles had gone into the paper, a former FBI agent named Frank Foster read about my case and called me. After doing his research and coming to his own conclusions, this man wrote the most beautiful article in the paper, and began to help me fight to overturn my sentence. One day, after I was sentenced, before I was scheduled to report, I got a call on the phone.

"Hello?"

"Yes, is this Ms. Carolyn Price?" he asked.

"Yes, who is this?" I replied.

"I'm Frank Foster, I'm a former FBI agent," he said.

"What is it?" I was really aggravated at first, thinking this was some other bad news.

"Don't be afraid of me," he said. "I want to help." I paused, and then I just started crying. I didn't know what to say.

"Ma'am, this man is a professional con artist. You might have been gullible, but you're not guilty," he said. "Out of the many people that he's done this to, nobody else has been arrested. I don't know why they came after you like this, but we're going to prove them wrong. You're a victim."

I didn't have any reason to believe him except that he sounded sincere.

"I have two children," I told him.

"Do you have them situated? Is there someone to keep them?" he asked.

"Yes, I do."

"Ok, well go down there, read, try not to stress over it, I guarantee you're not going to be down there for this amount of time that they said. We're going to get you home."

If God had not sent Frank Foster into my life, who knows how things could have gone. He was so helpful that I knew it could only have been through God that he came into my life.

He asked, "Is it alright if I call the paper?"

"I don't care," I told him. Anything that could possibly help, of course, I was all for it. I invited this man to go to church with me. A really good friend of mine, Lola, attended this church, and her mother was the pastor. Frank agreed to come with me. Service went as it usually did and nothing seemed out of the ordinary to me.

When we left, Frank asked, "Carolyn, how well do you know these people?"

"Oh, they're like family to me," I told him. "The pastor is like a mother to me and Lola is like a sister."

He looked directly at me and said, "That girl

envies you. She wants to be you. She'll take everything you've got if she gets the chance." I chuckled at this.

"No Frank, it's nothing like that," I didn't really pay it much mind at the time. Frank just sighed. In his eyes, I saw that he wanted to say more, but thought that it wouldn't do any good, and he was right.

I remember that they wanted me to report right after the new year began. This was a terrible time for me to leave. It had nothing to do with the holiday, or some New Year's Resolution, but about my family. Charmayne's birthday was on January 5th, and Dee's birthday was on January 6th. I didn't know if they would be lenient about it, because they sure were not lenient about sending me away for no reason in the first place. In the most firm, but polite way possible, I explained to them why I would really appreciate it if I could report later. It worked. They told me to report on January 12th.

That day, I had Chloe and Dee and I dropped them off at school that morning before I drove down there. I remember telling them to be good, and telling them to remember everything I had told them. I repeated a lot of those things. I sat in that car and looked at both of them with no idea of when I would see them again. That feeling is indescribable. They had a really hard time when I was left.

Being transported to the prison was a nerve-racking experience. I didn't know what to expect. Like most people, I had formed my opinions of prison from movies and television shows. Who would I be around? Where would I sleep? What would I eat? Would I have to protect myself? Some people are conditioned to go to prison because they choose a life of crime. In situations like that, they already know they are likely to end up there. They accept that fact as a certainty. For me, it was a shocking experience.

Nothing can take the place of being in your own home, and eating your own food, with your own family, so I don't want to make it seem like I didn't mind being in prison: I did mind. But when we arrived and I saw where I would be living, I was relieved! We were in a federal, minimum security prison that looked nothing like a prison.

You would have no idea it was a prison by just looking at it. The rooms were like hotel rooms. There were usually two people to each room, sometimes three. There were no bars or ugly stone walls. We had closets and dressers as you would in a college dorm room. We were not locked up. We could walk in and out of our rooms as we pleased. If someone wanted to escape from there, they would not have had to dig through some tunnel, or jump over a fence, they could have just walked away. It would have been as easy as a kid walking away from high school. On the inside, it really did not feel like a prison at all.

We went to school, we went to the beauty shop, we exercised and we ate good. We had a restaurant in there where we ate every day. We could order our own eggs, we could order our own meat, and almost whatever else you could imagine. It wasn't like you see in the movies with people walking through a cafeteria line with grey trays and people slapping scoops of food on top of them. People would actually drive up into the prison on accident because they thought it was a resort. "Where do I sign up?" or "Where's the leasing office?" People would actually ask that, ha!

We were free to move around as we liked. We didn't wait for someone to bring our mail to us and slide it through some slot. We would just walk to the box and get our mail. We would just go to one of the activity rooms to play cards if we wanted. We would go to the TV room to look at movies and sports. We watched all the Cowboys games, of course. We used to go for walks out on the yard or to the library. It really was more like a vacation resort. We did have a certain time to be in our room, but we could stay up as late as we wanted to once we were in there. I liked being in my room anyway. My name in there was Dallas, because I love the Cowboys so much. That's what everyone called me: Dallas.

I stayed in touch with Frank Foster and he always gave me updates on how things were going with my case. I was so grateful for him. I didn't have any money to give him for his trouble or anything to reward him with. He had his own reasons for doing it. That was between him and God, I suppose, but I was certainly thankful for it. I just knew that it could only be God that sent him to me.

I had a lot of help with keeping my personal business together. Karis stayed in touch and was really helpful with certain things. Judy helped me out tremendously as well. Besides checking on me, she helped out financially and gave some money to the kids. My friend Alice Jones, who used to work at the bank with me, also helped me out, and my friend Lola from church did as well. Lola sent a lot of letters and would always encourage me. I had a strong circle of people that really stood by me and made sure that things were taken care of, and I am forever grateful to them for that.

I had let Charmayne move into my house and take care of it for me while I was gone. I thought it would be helpful to both of us. I needed the house kept up and I figured it would help her out with having a place to stay. All she had to do was pay the mortgage for me so that I could keep the house until I got out. Lola was checking with her to make sure that it was being taken care of. I bought the house back in the 70's at a good price, so the mortgage was reasonable. It was slightly over four hundred dollars per month. One day, Lola came to the camp to visit me, and she was concerned.

"Carolyn, Charmayne hasn't been paying the mortgage," she explained. "You're behind a few months." I quite naturally panicked because that was my place of residence. Fighting to get out knowing I was innocent had already devastated me, so I really needed someone to stand by me. She made two separate visits, and what she told me was that she was going to take care of the house so that I wouldn't have any problems.

"I'll pay the mortgage," she said, "but I'm not going to pay it while she stays there." After speaking with my family and my daughter, there were times when Lola was in and out of the house unannounced and Charmayne was at the point where she just didn't want to keep dealing with it, not thinking about how valuable the house was to me at the time. She knew that I trusted Lola, so she just moved on.

Later on, Lola wrote me a letter and told me that she had a lady, who I would really love, who worked with her and would rent the house until I got home. That way the house would be kept up and then she could just transfer everything over to me when I got back. That was an ideal situation, because I needed someone responsible to take care of the house. I trusted Lola, and I told her that I would turn everything over to her. I made sure she got the title, and told her to keep it for me because Texas was a community state, and my ex-husband's name was still on the house as well. I didn't want him to take advantage of me being gone and decide to do something with the house in my absence.

I actually met some really nice women during

my time in prison. We did as much as we could to make the time pass. I have pictures from there that look like glamour shots. You would think we were on a cruise somewhere. I never could get comfortable enough to accept my sentence though. It made me wonder how many other innocent people were in prison. If it could happen to me, it certainly could happen to a lot of other people.

I continued to check in with Frank, and he assured me that he was making progress in his effort to get me out. I even received a message from the famous movie director Spike Lee when I was there. Can you imagine that? I have no idea how he heard about it. I guess my case had gone national. He had heard about me and reached out to give his support. That meant so much to me.

When the time drew near for Dee to graduate from high school, it took a toll on me. The thought of not being able to enjoy that moment with her was something that I didn't want to deal with. I decided to write a letter to the warden. I explained everything. I explained how Clara Jean's life was tragically taken away from her, and how I had raised her kids as my own. I explained how Verneana's life was taken in much the same way, and how I had taken Dee in the same way that I had taken her mother in. I explained how much it would mean to me if I could attend her graduation. I poured my heart into the letter and I waited for a response. When the response came, it was great news. I could go!

The permission was granted and she sent the proper forms down to the dorm to let them know. The lady in charge at the dorm didn't like it. She was something else! Her father worked there too. It was a family business for them, I suppose. There was nothing she could do about it though. I had to get ready, and I had to fill out a form with all the questions about who I would stay with and other information like that. Graduation would be that Saturday, so I had to have somebody pick me up that Friday and I had to be back that Sunday night. I went in there ready to go. She gave me my information and I prepared to leave. Even though I had been told a day and time when I had to return, I wanted to be sure, so I asked, "What day am I supposed to be back?" I didn't want any misunderstandings over a technicality.

"You have a whole week," she said.

I was floored. In that situation, I can't describe what those extra days felt like. For that week, things were like normal again.

One day, I spoke to my neighbor, who was also a pastor, and he told me that my pastor, Lola's mother, had visited his church and ministered one day. That was great, but it was what he said next that was strange.

"I think her daughter is moving in your house," he said referring to Lola. I didn't really know what was going on. I know originally she mentioned that she might rent it out to someone, but I didn't know. I just really wanted to get home to find out what was going on for myself.

One day, seemingly out of the blue, I got the news I was waiting for. My release had been granted and I would be going home. Thank God for sending Frank Foster as a guardian angel for me! I was told to expect leave in 2-3 months. 33 ½ months? No, that decision was for God to make, not man. I would have rather left that day, but at least now I knew the day was coming.

I walked into the prison on a cold day in January, and it was a mild November morning when I walked out. My life and everything that I had worked so hard for had been put on hold. I was really anxious to get back and pick up where I had left off. Thanks to Frank, and his diligent effort on my behalf, I walked away with the conviction wiped from my record, ready to reset my life.

7 BLIND SIDE BETRAYAL

As they arrive and pull into the gates at the stadium, Ms. Price gives an enthusiastic greeting to the parking lot attendant. "Good morning! What game is this?" Obviously she knows, but can't resist pulling the joke out again.

"Uh...it's Detroit," the attendant responds.

"They're still in the NFL?" Ms. Price feigns surprise at the thought.

"This is the last year that they're going to be in the league," he plays along.

"Are you kidding me? It's really Detroit? Y'all don't hold me up now." She extends a parking pass to the man. He scans it and returns it to her.

"Thank you baby, "Preciate y'all."

"Have fun," he offers.

"Thanks honey," Ms. Price drives towards the front of the stadium.

Pulling into her parking spot, she begins to gather her things for the tailgate festivities, and the game. Another attendant approaches the car to offer her assistance if needed.

"Ok, let me get my ticket out," she says reaching into the center console of her car.

"This is Detroit, they keep saying. I don't even believe it.

They're not still in the NFL." "Unfortunately so," says the second attendant.

"Aw y'all are just making up stuff, y'all always do this. Why does Dallas do this?" Ms. Price asks. "They just make up stuff." After retrieving her ticket and other belongings, Ms. Price suddenly exits the car very quickly. She doesn't hear the attendant who's trying to say something else to her.

"Let me get on in here baby. See you after the game." She rushes by and out amongst the other fans who've arrived early to tailgate and fellowship before the game begins.

As Ms. Price stands and talks to a friend about possibly flying to an away game to see a former Cowboys player, a tall blonde-haired man approaches to greet her.

"Hello," he says.

"Hi, how are you?" she asks.

"I've got you on my Facebook," he begins. "This is my first time meeting you."

Ms. Price erupts into a loud laugh, "he says we're friends on Facebook. Do I ever tell you hi?"

"Yes," the man replies.

"Well it's good to meet you in person darling," she tells the man. "Let's move it! We got a game to play." As the time draws nearer for kickoff of the game, a flip switches and Ms. Price goes into another gear.

"Y'all, let's go! Hey, hey Earline, let's go. Cynthia,

Helga, let's go." Along with her other friends, she is also now accompanied by another friend, Helga. At every home game, Ms. Price is pressed up against the rail, waiting to greet the players as they run out of the tunnel and onto the field. She refuses to miss this part of the game experience and is quickly losing patience for anyone who might cause her to.

Walking towards the gate, they approach the players' parking lot in front of the stadium. Beautiful, expensive cars of all makes and models are parked in the lot and fans stand around taking pictures of the cars.

"That's Dez' car right there," says Cynthia.

"Look at this one," replies Helga.

"I'm going to take a picture real quick," Cynthia says. As Cynthia and Helga pause to take a couple of pictures, Ms. Price keeps walking. Earline follows closely behind. As Ms. Price knifes through the crowd, Earline walks briskly to keep up.

"They're back there somewhere," Earline says. "I don't see 'em."

"That's ok, I told them to come on, Ms. Price is not going to wait all day darling. When I say come on, that's what I mean."

About fifteen minutes later, after they've made the trek up and down several escalators, through several hallways and downstairs to the lower level of the stadium, Earline is on the phone.

"Ok, I can't hardly hear you," Earline says. "I'll tell her." Earline hangs up the phone. They said they can't get down here. They don't have passes and they stopped them at the gate.

"I told them to come on, I'll send someone to get them at halftime, but I'm not about to miss the players coming out," Ms. Price says. *"They'll learn next time that when I say I'm ready to move, I mean it."*

I was so thrilled to be free and on my way back to Dallas, I think I was shaking. The excitement was overwhelming. I imagined what I would do when I got home. But as the saying goes, if it ain't one thing, it's another. In this case, the other thing was another betrayal: this time not by a stranger, but by someone who was close to me and that I trusted very much: Lola. Trying to keep my house out of foreclosure, I thought I had did the right thing by giving her the deed to my home while she kept the payments up for me. That was a horrible mistake. When I got home and I told her I was ready to move back in, she started ignoring my calls and avoiding me.

It turns out that she had gotten my ex-husband to sign off on his part of the deed to the home, and he turned the rest over to her. When I asked Willie about it, he said that she had given him one thousand dollars and he thought that she was keeping the house for me. He also knew her and her mom very well, and he thought that she was helping me. He said he didn't have a reason to be suspicious because of how close we were.

Charmayne told me that she said she had power of attorney over my affairs, but I never gave her that. I went downtown to check it out and there was an order for power of attorney, but the signature on it wasn't mine. She had literally stolen the house from me like it was a television set or a lamp or just some random object. She took everything I had.

I had bought Dee a new, beautiful bedroom set and she took that. All she gave me was a bag of clothes, and nothing in there even belonged to me. It was terrible. It was just her junk and old leftover stuff, some that use to belong to the kids, and things like that. I confronted her about it and demanded that she turn the house back over to me.

With her mother, my pastor, standing right by her side she told me, "give me twenty thousand dollars and then maybe we can talk." Twenty thousand? I didn't have twenty dollars. I had just made it back home.

I was floored. It's amazing how sometimes people can see things so clearly around us that we can't. God will put people in our lives to tell us things. We just have to listen. Frank Foster's words from a couple of years prior replayed in my mind.

"Carolyn, how well do you know these people? That girl envies you. She wants to be you. She'll take everything you've got if she has the chance."

"For what?" I asked. You were supposed to be helping me!

"It's a business deal," she replied. Imagine the betrayal. It was terrible enough for her to do this in the first place, but for her mother to be the pastor of my church, and to stand by and encourage it, that was a level of deceit that I couldn't make sense of. That was evil. A pastor is the person who I should be able to turn to for counsel when someone pulls something like this on me, but she was a part of the scheme. I was completely outdone. She actually got really sick not too long after that and passed away.

I stood looking at this girl in disbelief. I didn't know her. I was so heartbroken because she had been like a sister to me. She wrote me letters that helped me get through while I was away. She loved me, or at least I thought she did. She was always saying, "Sis, hang in there." She was always supportive. She was someone that I could always lean on, or so it seemed. Looks can be so deceiving.

That's why I'm a little bit more standoffish nowadays. I've been hurt so much that it made me more careful about people. I really hate that because I was always so open and I met so many genuine people that way. You can never completely change, so I'm still that way, but there's always that caution sign in the back of my mind based on what Lola did. There were people who were really, really mean to me and I didn't know it was all because of jealousy. I didn't have sense enough to know that I was all that, ha! I had no idea.

At this point, I basically had nothing. Besides the house, there were the material items as well. I had beautiful clothes and always took pride in that. This girl went through my clothes and took what she wanted.

I didn't have anywhere to go, so I had to bounce around and live with different family members and friends. Some of my family members were not very nice to me, and then some of my younger relatives didn't want me around because of what they were doing. They were smoking their marijuana and stuff like that, and they didn't want me around that. I believe that's a good reflection on me that they didn't want me around that. It means that they knew I had certain standards that I would uphold. I never did any type of drugs, and I was always against that.

I tried staying with a friend that I had known for a while and had helped out quite a bit, but that turned into another negative experience because she was an alcoholic. I wanted to stay and be there for her, but I couldn't take staying there and seeing what she was doing to herself.

I called my goddaughter Karis. "I'm so tired," I told her. "I'm just fed up."

"What is it Price?" she asked. That's what she always called me and still does to this day, simply "Price."

"I'm just tired," I told her. "I'm never going to get my house back. I'm just tired."

"You want to come live with me?" Karis asked.

"I can?" I never liked feeling like I was inconveniencing someone.

"Of course you can," she answered. At that low point, she was there for me. She knew my heart and how much I had helped everyone around me when I was able, so I guess she couldn't imagine not helping me. She came, picked me up and took me to her house.

I was placed in such a position through this adversity that I had no choice but to go forward. There was nothing for me to look back for. There were so many things that had not been packed up, and a lot of it just sat outside for the garbage man to pick up. Lola did at least put some stuff in storage. But let me give you an example of how God works: I was over to my sister's apartment one day and there was a girl over there who lived across the hall from her. I didn't know this girl at all. So on this particular day when I met this girl, out of the blue she said, "I saw some pictures of you."

"Excuse me?" I replied. I didn't have any idea what she was talking about. Well, when Charmayne lived in an apartment and had some of my stuff, she moved away and left it, so people went around collecting this stuff. It just so happens that this girl had a red frame with a picture of her in it.

"This is my frame," I said. I knew because it was a unique frame and I recognized it. "These are mines. I'm getting ready to take them. Do you want me to take your pictures out?"

"Yes, that's fine. You can have them," she answered, "and I have your pictures too." This girl still had my pictures that are sitting in my house to this day. These are testimonies. I don't have to make this stuff up. Sometimes, it's so hard for me to believe that people don't believe God will do things like that. What are the chances of me coincidentally meeting this girl and getting some important pictures back that way?

When I was ready to begin looking for my own apartment, I tried to gather as many of my things as I could scrape together. I was staying with Alice at that point. I had moved in with her after I stayed with Karis for a while.

I said to Dee, "I'm coming down there to get my microwave." That was another thing I hadn't gotten back since I had been home. Back in those days, microwaves were a lot more expensive than they are now: four, five, maybe even six hundred dollars depending on what you bought, so I needed that one. I didn't have money to just go buy another one.

I went to get the microwave and Charmayne said, "If that was Chloe, you wouldn't take it. I don't know why you want to take it from me." She turned things like that into a competition.

"I'm trying to get something together," I told her. "I don't have nowhere to go so I'm trying to get me a little apartment." She acted up and fussed about it, so I left and went back to Alice's house. Not too long afterwards, I got a call from Dee.

"Mama, something just happened. That microwave you came over to get just blew up! We had to call the firemen and everything," she explained.

"Are you kidding me?" I asked. She was not kidding. So I guess like they say, what's meant for you is meant for you.

Naturally, besides a roof over my head, I also had to figure out where I would work. I had a couple of offers to go back into banking, but there was a sour taste in my mouth from everything that I had gone through. I didn't want to go back to that. I wanted to go in a new direction. In the meantime, I got by on temporary jobs and the blessings of others. There were people that were so nice to me to the point that it was just breathtaking. One man owned an air conditioning business, another was an attorney, and both of those guys donated things to me to help me transition back to my life. Everybody was giving me things when I got home, whether it was a few hundred dollars, or items that I needed for my home. I didn't want for anything.

I was looking for a permanent place to work, and the search led me to a hospital agency. It was a place where I could help out, because I knew the girls who owned it, but it wasn't a permanent position. I had such a warm personality and I knew so many people that it was a natural fit for me. I was able to communicate with the doctors, social workers, nurses and patients with no problem.

One day, my friend Cassandra said, "why don't you just go to school so you can make a career out of it?" I knew the Lord wanted me to go on and get my license because at the first agency I was working at, they accidentally printed RN behind my name. I took that as a sign, but I said to myself, "I'm not going through all those years of college to be a registered nurse." I just wanted enough training to work in the field.

Most of what I knew about the field up to that point was because I had spent a lot of time around a woman named Francis Stiggers, and this woman was truly a genius. She knew so much about the medical field, and she taught me so much. I give her all the credit in the world for that. She knew so much about different medicines, what they were for and why they were useful in different situations.

Francis had the same idea about me going to school. She told me, "If you get your CNA license, with all your knowledge, you can do just about whatever you want to do." I took that advice and did just that. Eventually, I ran into Mrs. Massey, one of my teachers from back at Booker T. Washington High School. She became one of my patients. It was gratifying to be able to take care of her after she had done so much for me when I was young. I felt like I was returning the favor.

Ms. Stiggers and Cassandra were a lot alike personality-wise. They were both laid-back, really sweet people. Cassandra's son's name was Kevin and he played for the Cowboys for a while. I had met her on a previous job that we were on and left together once the company folded.

I decided to just get my CNA: Certified Nursing Assistant License. I didn't want to be in school too long. I just wanted enough schooling to have some medical knowledge, and be able to get back to work.

At this point, several of the other girls and I had started drawing unemployment. That helped me to make it through that period. One day, Cassandra came to me with another idea. "Carolyn, I think I have something you really need to check out."

"What?" I was curious.

"I know a guy who started an agency, but he really needs someone to help him," she explained. "I think he needs somebody exactly like you."

It sounded like a great opportunity, but by that point, things had turned around and that wasn't the only job offer I had. I had options at that point. I went to see Mr. Alfred Akinola, the guy she was telling me about, and he was actually just getting started. He had about twelve patients, and he definitely needed help with them.

I saw him and just thought, "Lord, what should I do? Should I help this man or what?" I started helping him, and he offered me a salary. It was pretty nice, but not what I had been making. It was really close to home though, just a few minutes away, so that made the difference. I started working for Mr. Alfred and God continued to bless me. My salary continued to increase and I kept getting raises as the business grew. Eventually, I became the manager of the facility.

I had finally got a place to call my own: a one bedroom apartment. This was around '98 or '99. Talk about downsizing. At least it had two closets. This is where I met my godson, Audante: he was my neighbor. I had my grandkids with me, and he had his little boy with him. He was going through a custody fight in court for his little boy at the time. We talked about our situations and of course, The Cowboys. We had a lot of laughs and we were just there for each other at a time when we both needed somebody. I helped him out a whole lot and he helped me a whole lot. As is the story with my life, he and his wife Janean became part of my family and we're there for each other as if it was always that way.

I came home one day and there was a card from the FBI in my door. I called my friend and told her about it, because that's not something you get every day. Then I figured, if there was a problem and they wanted me for something, they wouldn't just bring a card to the house and leave it: they would just come in and get me. I had been through it before.

So, I called the number and the guy said, "Hello, Carolyn?"

I said, "This is Ms. Price."

He started in asking me questions about Fritz and some scheme he was up to. I guess he had gotten out of prison and gone right back to his old ways. He wanted to know if I had heard from him or was dealing with him.

"If you ever call my house and question me about some idiotic things like that again," I told him, "you'll be in big trouble. Huge trouble. Don't ever call my house again."

When God delivered me from that situation, a lot of it just left my mind. Sometimes, when you go through things like that, they stay on your mind and you think about them over and over again. Sometimes you go through something like that and don't think about it at all. You just block it from your mind and leave it behind. That's the way it is with me. That's something I don't think about at all.

I was slowly building myself back up and recovering from everything that had happened. It's like I was still getting used to the fact that so many people had taken advantage of me. It was almost like having post-traumatic stress disorder. The bottom line is that I was always a very popular, well-liked person in whatever capacity of life I was in whether it was banking, or another place where I was working, or a church, or just in the community as a whole. I was popular in the same way in school, but at this particular point in my life, everyone knew that I was going through a hard time. I was surprised to find out that I really had people close to me who would want to take advantage of that. I didn't understand it at the time and it's still hard to.

So, when they tried to kick me when I was down, they had no idea it would come to this, that I would get back up and stand even taller. They knew me, and how I took care of my business, so they knew I would get a place to stay, but figured it would be something basic and sufficient. I'm sure they assumed that I would get a car also, but nothing too nice. They knew I would always keep my hair fixed and look alright but never, ever did they think I would come out the way I did: a new and improved, far better version of myself.

I've had people, Christian people, ask me, "how did this happen?" I say, "It's Jesus," and I can give you examples.

One Saturday morning, I was riding past an area where some new homes had been built. A woman told me that the houses had been built for specific owners, but that either the financing had fallen through on them, or the contracts just didn't go through for some reason.

There was a two-story house that would have been about two or three hundred dollars more per month than I wanted to pay, but I didn't want that for myself. I figured, I didn't need that much house. I asked to look at the house next door, which was a three bedroom. But then, I noticed that the house on the corner was available: a four bedroom. I liked it. *I'll take the four bedroom.* I wrote them a five hundred dollar check to start the process, and went back to work. One Saturday, I called my godson and I called my granddaughter, and I said, "I want you to come ride somewhere with me.

I brought them right to the house that I'm

sitting in now.

"Wow, you've already been doing this haven't you?" Dante asked. There wasn't much to do, besides be blessed.

"I have found a place to stay, and I'm moving here!" I claimed it and it was mine.

When you receive blessings like that, you shouldn't mind passing them onto others. I had a Mercury Topaz that was the first car I bought when I came home. I used to let Dee's husband drive it, and I basically just had it sitting at the house parked. In the apartments, they didn't like cars just constantly sitting with no one driving them. I was going to just stick it in the garage, but instead, I sold it to him for little or nothing. I knew I wanted something else. I just didn't know what.

One day, I was driving out I-30 East, and I was noticing cars. Nowadays, cars just seem to look more and more alike regardless of the make, and sometimes you can't really tell what it is until you look at the emblem. You can see a car that looks like a Lexus, but it's something about all these cars that has that look until you see that sign. I had never liked Cadillacs, and those types of cars, because they were just so bulky to me.

On this day, I was riding down the expressway, and I saw this fabulous-looking car on a billboard. *Wow, what is that?* It just looked beautiful. *That's a Cadillac?* I couldn't believe it, but all of a sudden a Cadillac wasn't so bad. This one was for me.

I was driving my little Mercury Topaz and I made up my mind to go and drive that car. I went to the lot, and let them know that I was interested. I test drove that car. I left and went about my business, and the next thing you know, they delivered that car to my job.

After I had been working for Mr. Alfred awhile, I saw how well the office was doing and I said to him, "Papa, why don't you open up a place in Fort Worth?" I started explaining why I thought that would be a good idea. He nodded to let me know he was listening, but didn't say much about it. I didn't know if he was really paying me much attention or not.

Not long after that, he came back to me and said, "Ok, I'm going to open a Fort Worth office." So, I flew to Houston with him and helped him get that done. He had to go through orientation classes and complete a detailed process. From there, he just kept going and kept expanding.

He went through a lot of his own trials with his first wife and his two boys. One of his boys works with him now. I would always just tell him, "God will work it out." The business flourished more and more and I felt blessed to be a part of it. Accepting a position with him turned out to be the best decision that I could have made.

Because of that decision, I was able to help my kids more, which meant a whole lot to me. There were a number of issues going on with them by this point. My granddaughter, Chloe, was pregnant, and she was having thoughts about whether she wanted to have the child. She worried about whether or not she would be in a position to handle everything that comes with that. She's married now, but she wasn't then.

"I don't want this baby, Mama," she said.

"Abortion is not a form of protection," I told her. "The protection was supposed to come beforehand. So what we're going to do is take care of this baby." That baby is almost grown now. She was joking with me not too long ago.

"Don't kill my grandbaby, don't kill my grand baby!" she mocked me.

"Girl, what are you talking about?" I asked her.

"That was you," she laughed.

I didn't even know she remembered that, but I was serious!

Lola's son sent me a message on Facebook not too long ago that said, "I will always love you." We used to call each other "Sis." What happened should have never happened, and everyone has to reap what they sow. It's funny how everything turned out so good for me, on the heels of so many people doing so much bad to me.

PRICELESS DREAM

8 THE DALLAS COWBOYS #1 FAN

"Give 'em some more! Don't give 'em no air! Keep 'em under the water!" Ms. Price leads the cheers in the section directly behind the Cowboys' bench during the game. Periodically, fans make their way next to her during timeouts, or breaks in the action to introduce themselves and take pictures. On this day, Ms. Price has taken a young fan under her wing, and told her that she's training her to take over when she's done. She's a young, blonde girl, not quite a teenager, in attendance with her family.

"Yes! Keep 'em under the water," the young fan repeats.

"Jay-SUN! Jason Whit-TUN!" she screams at Cowboys' tight end Jason Whitten. *"Get 'em Jason! Don't give 'em no air now."* A familiar chant used in stadiums throughout the country begins and Ms. Price gives her young protégé instructions.

"When they do that, I want you to clap, ok?" The young fan nods and begins to clap to the beat. A short, stocky fan with dark, brown hair walks up and pats Ms. Price on the shoulder.

"Hey Ms. Price," she gives him a hug. *"What's up*

baby! What's going on?

"How you doing?" he inquires.

"I'm fine," Ms. Price replies. "She's in training," Ms. Price says of the young fan. "Watch this. "TONY ROMO!" Ms. Price yells.

"Tony Romo!" the young fan does her best, but sounds as if her young vocal chords may give out at any minute trying to keep up with the bellows of Ms. Price.

"GO GET 'EM!"

"GO GET 'EM!" She lets out her best high-pitched simulation of Ms. Price.

"JASON WHITTEN!"

"JASON WHITTEN!" They go back and forth like this periodically throughout the game. It's easy to see who's used to being around Ms. Price and who isn't. Those who've never been around her alternate between watching the game and watching her to see what she'll say and do next.

After the game, the mood is much different. The Cowboys lost a big lead in the second half as quarterback Tony Romo threw a pair of interceptions, and the Lions staged an epic comeback. Like a true matriarch in any family, Ms. Price does not want to hear anyone being too critical of Romo.

"Like that guy said, Tony threw those interceptions, you can't take that back, but that defense should have been tight like they were in that first and second quarter. They wasn't doing nothing either, so you can't put everything on Tony. That's why they call it a team."

Most of the fans have filed out of the stadium, but some stick around near the field to try to get a moment with the players as they exit the locker room. As several of owner Jerry

Jones' grandchildren emerge from the tunnel, Ms. Price reacts as if they are family members that she hasn't seen in a while, and the response is mutual.

"Hey!"

"How are you?" The tallest of the group asks.

"Y'all are getting so doggone big. My God. Ms. Price is doing good." She gives each of the three teens a hug, one by one.

"Hey, hey baby! Are y'all on my Facebook?" "Yes," the reply in unison.

"Wait a minute, I need to get a picture with all of y'all."

As they stand around taking pictures, she reminisces about them as if they're pictures in a photo album that she's flipping through.

"He plays football too," she pats the tallest of the grandchildren on the back. "What position do you play baby?"

"Strong Safety."

"When we were winning Super Bowls, he was the baby," she explains. "I always tell him he's going to be the next in line after Stephen."

"This is Jerry's daughter's baby," she says wrapping her arm around his shoulder and pulling him close. "This baby has been like this since the day he was born. He is such a unique guy. And this one here..."

As people will tell you, I inherited my position as The Dallas Cowboys #1 Fan from my friend, Crazy Ray. I was always there and the players had recognized me for many, many years before the media really got a hold of my story, but Ray was older than me. The same way that the camera people make sure to find me now, and all of the other fans come up to me to take pictures and ask me to sign autographs, that was how the people responded to Crazy Ray since back in the early days.

His real name was Wilford Jones, but everyone knew him as Crazy Ray. Crazy Ray was the Cowboys' unofficial mascot since the early 60's. I was at the games at that time, but we were young: I was still a teenager. Ray was much older and already a grown man at that point. We all loved him and he entertained everybody. How could we not love someone showing that much love for the Cowboys and having so much fun while he did it? He was at all of the games, blowing his whistle and drawing attention to his love for the Cowboys. He would run around on his little toy hobby horse and the kids would just crack up.

Ray used to do a lot for the kids. He really loved the kids and the kids really loved Ray. He would do magic tricks and create little balloon animals like they do sometimes at birthday parties.

My friend Fred worked with Ray down at the Sheraton Hotel. Ray shined shoes there and Fred worked in the laundry. In the mid 90's, Ray's health started to fail. He had diabetes and he had issues with his heart as well. He had his leg amputated in 1997. Ray loved the Cowboys so much that he would still attend games, but obviously he couldn't do all the things that he loved to do. Coincidentally, it was around this time that more and more people recognized me.

My voice could always be heard over everyone else's and I always had my Cowboys accessories on from head to toe. Like I said before, I was always a really popular person in the community already outside of anything having to do with football. The players and the fans had been gravitating towards me as early as the 70's because you couldn't help it: I was everywhere. The difference was, now it was more of the fans from out of town and away games that started to recognize me too. Not only did I go to the games, but I went to training camp, and any other event where our players would be. You would always catch me at the front of the line whenever our players ran out of the tunnel and onto the field. All of this was long before Jerry Jones bought the team, but once he took over, everything changed. Jerry thinks big when it comes to everything, and we saw that right away.

It was really great being around my Cowboys in the '90's and getting a chance to see them enjoy their success. We had some really great teams at the end of the 1960's, and that carried over into the 70's, but it was like something was missing in the 80's. We couldn't get back over that hump. To see the guys come back after hitting rock bottom in 1989, when we went 1-15, was a thrill to see.

Those teams had a reputation for being wild,

but I don't think they were any wilder than the average young, famous guys with money would be. They weren't all like that. Troy Aikman was a really nice guy. He was really reserved and laid back. I looked at him almost like a politician. He knew what to say and how to carry himself as the quarterback of America's team. That's an important position to have. Larry Allen and Darryl Johnston, who everybody knows as Moose, were both the same way. They were pretty laid back. You always heard a lot more about the flamboyant ones who did all the partying, but you didn't hear about the others as much. But it's no secret that a lot of that went on.

The first time that I met Jerry Jones in person was really brief. During the Super Bowl run, there was a place called the Coral that we used to go to after the games. A lot of fans would go there and the players would come and hang with the people there. It was right across from the old stadium. One day, Mr. Jones came out of the stadium walking over to the Coral. I remember it so vividly because it was my sister Sandra's birthday. She was born on November 1st.

"Oh Sandra, there's Jerry Jones!" I said. He walked right up with a bunch of people around him.

"Yeah, yeah, baby," he said smiling.

"Mr. Jones, they used to laugh at us when we were 1-15," I yelled. "Look at us now!"

"They're not laughing now are they?" Those were the very words he spoke and I'll never forget that. We didn't really talk to him too much that day because that was during the peak of our Super Bowl run. It was really hectic around him.

We had won the Super Bowl after the 1992 and 1993 seasons, and then again following the 1995 season. After the last Super Bowl in '95, we were still hanging around the top of the league in '96 and '97 but we couldn't break through. We were still in the hunt, and a really good team, but just not quite as powerful. One day, I was standing on the sideline in my usual place to greet the players when they were coming out of the tunnel. I was very excited, as usual. Darren Woodson came over and gave me a hug, spoke to me briefly and Channel 5 aired that clip later. Charmayne was there with me that day. I was screaming and yelling as I usually do. It's so strange when I'm down there, like an out of body experience. I just get so caught up in everything: all of the players coming by slapping my hand, responding when I yell at them. I had no idea that Mr. Jones was paying attention.

Next thing I know, he came strolling up to me. I was so excited when he came over. He stood and spoke for a couple of minutes and his son Stephen was with him. It was like I was in a big dream and I came home and I was telling everyone, "Guess who I talked to? Jerry Jones!"

"Yeah, that's nice," and "oh ok," were the type of reactions I got. Clearly they were not as excited as me. But things began to happen more after that. I was at another game, and at that point, they would let VIPs come down on the field, but they would rope us off in a way that we couldn't interfere with the players. I didn't care what they did, I was going to find a way to get close to the players so I could talk with them. This time, we got a chance to talk to Jerry for a lot longer. I was down on the field screaming my head off and Stephen came over to me.

Stephen said, "Wait right there, don't move." He went and got Jerry and brought him over there and he stood and spoke with us. He was really down to earth. This time, he asked how long I had been coming to the games, and how often I came to the games. I thought maybe they just think, "Oh, there's that crazy lady down there." I didn't know they knew me by name, or knew, "that's Ms. Price."

It turned out that they really knew who I was because Karis worked as a manicurist. It just so happened that she was Gene Jones' manicurist and routinely did her nails. Gene Jones is Jerry's wife. One day, Gene was in the beauty shop and Karis had a book with my picture on it sitting nearby.

Gene noticed it, pointed and said, "That lady right there is something else."

"That's my godmother," Karis told her.

"You're kidding," Gene replied. She knew who I was, and that conversation led to a lot of other conversations. That's how I first met Gene: through Karis.

I remember one time at training camp, Jerry

Jones was walking down the sideline at training camp signing autographs.

"Come on baby," he looked right at me and waved for me to walk with him.

"I'll walk with you!" I was thrilled. I hung out with him for the rest of the time he was down on the field that day until he left. You would think I would get used to it. I have gotten more used to it as time went on, but I love my 'Boys so much that it's still a thrill. Jerry takes a lot of criticism from people in the media, fans and from a lot of people who don't even matter. But if you really get to know somebody, you'll be a little bit more careful what you say and think about them.

A lot of people haven't had a chance to sit and talk and get to know Jerry like that. I don't like to be boastful or brag, but I've had an opportunity that not many people get, and I'm grateful. I can actually call him a friend. I don't ever take anything that someone else says about somebody as concrete, I didn't even do that with my mother. I've always been a person of my own mind. Now, I'll listen, and I may say, "Wow, that's hard for me to believe because Mama wouldn't lie to me," but I still form my own opinion about people.

So, when Jerry first got here and there was the big controversy with the firing of Tom Landry, I knew it was business, and I knew it was more to it than the media was saying. Coach Landry had been the Cowboys' coach since the team began playing in the 60's. The fans loved him because The Cowboys have always been like a family, and he was the head of it.

Of course, if you've been around someone for nearly 30 years, you're going to be really attached to them. Jerry Jones believed it was best to start fresh with a new coach, and hired Jimmy Johnson, who was coaching The University of Miami at that time. The controversy came because people didn't feel that he treated Coach Landry with the respect that he deserved on the way out the door. I knew that he just didn't come up here and say, "You know what, you're fired. That's it, you're out of here." It was more to it than that, but that's the way they made it look.

Tom Landry was a great coach for a long time. With the type of life that I've experienced, it's easy for me to see and accept the fact that things are not going to be the same forever. Things happen. I've heard Mr. Jones say that if he had to do it again, he might do it differently.

I think all of us have experienced that in life: doing something one way and thinking later on that we could have done it differently. I don't think there was any bias involved. I think it was really just business and him trying to think of how to make the Cowboys better. A lot of people in the city were hurt by it though. I like to think that the ceremony a couple of years later when they inducted Coach Landry into the Cowboys Ring of Honor smoothed over some of the bad feelings. It was a huge event. I had a chance to be there for that. So many of the players were on stage with him. It was really great to see.

Another time, I was on the field cheering years ago and Jerry Jones came over to us. "Girl, I'll tell you. You fire me up," he said. He told me to come with him, and he took me on the bus with him to meet his friends. I didn't even know they paid attention to me, but they all knew who I was too. Another time, he took me out in the middle of the field with him, holding my hand, as everyone looked on.

"Ok, Jerry. I don't like being out here," I told him. "They're too rough."

"Aw hush," he said, "you've been hollering louder than anybody since you been out here. Don't act scared now."

People have different opinions about different things and I can't judge a person by what someone else thinks. A lot of people think Jerry has made bad decisions at times, but I think mostly people just don't know the whole story. The game is played on the field and it takes concentration. Our players just have to remember: they don't want you to win.

The people out there feel like, "who are you that everybody loves you so?" "Why do you get to be America's team?" That's the attitude of the average player who plays for other teams. If they played the whole season with the same motivation for their own success, instead of worrying about Dallas, maybe they wouldn't be sitting at home in January.

Around this time, I noticed the cameramen started to come up to me more and more. A lot more people began to tell me, "I saw you on TV." One morning, I was sitting at my desk at work and I was told, "Channel 4 said they would like to come to your house and film you." Come to my house and film me? Sure! I was ready. I let them see how diehard I really am.

When Michael Irvin got in his legal situation in 1996, it broke it my heart. He was found in a hotel room with drugs and faced criminal charges. We didn't know if he would have to go to prison, or how it would affect his career as a whole. I was very worried about him.

David Wells is Michael's security guy officially, but really he's his good friend. I met David Wells back in 1989 when I was still working for the bank. As I said before, I used to come into contact with so many people in the community at that position and I was just well-known for being a people person. One day, I met David at the bank and we began talking. Of course, me being me, the conversation turned to the Cowboys. I let him know how big of a fan I was. He told me that he worked with Michael Irvin as his security. Michael was still fairly new to the team at that point: he had been in the league for about a year or two.

Michael Irvin was known as "The Playmaker." He eventually teamed up with Troy Aikman and

Emmitt Smith and they returned our team to glory, where we belonged. Michael was there first though. He came to the league from The University of Miami with a reputation for making plays and he lived up to it. I've been such a big Cowboys fan all my life that when somebody asks who my favorite player is, I hate to choose between all of those players. I love so many of them, but people who really know me will tell you: Michael Irvin is my all-time favorite Cowboy.

That summer in '89, David invited me down to training camp in Austin, Texas. This was a turning point in my time as a Cowboys fan. Before that, I was always around and players noticed me, mostly because of my loud voice and my dedication. I was the fan who was always there at the front of the crowd, outside of the rope. David is the one who invited me in and first allowed me to get on the inside of that rope: up close and personal with the players and the team. Once I got on that side, I never went back.

During the trial in '96, I became almost like a part of the legal team. I used vacation days from my job, and I made sure I was there to support him.

No matter who I'm around, they all know how I feel about the Cowboys. So, it's not a surprise if I say I'm doing something related to them. I just told my administrator at that time that I was going to take my vacation.

"You're using your vacation time for that?" he asked.

"Yes, I am," why wouldn't I? I can remember seeing myself on the news one night walking out of the courtroom with Michael. Karis was watching TV with me.

"Whoa, Price! You got in on that one didn't you?" We sat there and laughed. Michael's sisters thanked me for being there every day. I just really cared about him and tried to be there for him like I would anyone I cared for.

When they moved, I moved. When they came in the courtroom, I came in. When they left, I left. I mainly helped David out since he had so much to be responsible for. I just tried to take a lot of that load off him. It was serious business to me. Inside the courtroom, I became almost like part intern, part security guard. If Michael, David, or anybody on the legal team needed food, something to drink, or anything of that nature, I would get it for them. When any of the fans who crowded around the courtroom tried to get too close, I would move them out of the way. Other players came to show support. Troy Aikman was there, and of course, people constantly tried to get close to him to get pictures and autographs and I would block them.

"Uh-uh, get back," I would tell them. "They are not here for that right now. This is court." I helped to keep the media away also. At such a serious time as that, they just really did not want to be bothered. I made sure that they weren't as much as I could. The people around there didn't know who I was. They didn't know if I was someone's mother or what.

When they would break for lunch, they would all leave together to eat. One day, Royce West, one of his attorneys stopped as they walked past on the way out.

"Ms. Price, you want to come with us?" he asked.

"Naw, I'd rather just wait here until y'all get back," I told him. And that's what I would do. When Michael would come back in, he would just wink at me or nod or something, and I would just look at him and nod as if to say, "It's going to be alright."

He ended up getting a plea deal and was able to avoid going to prison. He had to pay a fine and do community service hours. He was suspended for the first five games of that season. That season was the last of that era where we were really in the hunt to get back to the Super Bowl.

The next season, we went 6-10 and that run was officially over. You can trace the end of that era back to when Michael got hurt. When he got injured in Philadelphia, he was never the same after that. On what was a routine play, he suffered a spinal injury. The fans in Philadelphia actually cheered while he was down on the field. I couldn't believe the people were actually cheering while he was laid out on the field unable to move. That's rare. Most fans show good sportsmanship with it comes to injuries, no matter how nasty they might be about anything else. To this day, that's one of the most infamous moments in NFL history. People still talk about how disrespectful those fans were to one of the greatest players ever.

Right after that was when a lot of the other players started retiring, and it was never the same again for that particular group. After Troy, we had trouble finding a quarterback we could stick with for the long haul.

When my brother Willie took sick, I would take him to get his treatments, but he would make sure not to miss a Lakers game on television. He loved the Lakers like I love the Cowboys: well, maybe not quite that much. I don't know if that's possible. As he became more ill, I couldn't stand to see him just sit around and do nothing while his condition got worse. I decided to take Willie to training camp with me so he could get away.

His wife told me, "You can't take him to training camp with you."

"Yes I can," I shot back. I didn't want him to just sit around and stop living. I felt like that was only a small step away from giving up, and I would not allow him to do that. That was when Emmitt was still playing, and my brother really loved Emmitt. When I left the room, I made sure that he had his medicine and everything, and we headed to training camp. During the times when he felt up to it, I would take him down on the field with me.

I have a lot of nephews and nieces, but

Willie's first born, Sonya, has a special bond with me and we've grown closer and closer throughout the years.

When I returned home from training camp, I was exhausted. All of a sudden, my phone was ringing off the hook and everyone was excited because I was on the front page of the *Dallas Morning News*. There I was, hugging Emmitt, and it was such a beautiful picture.

One time, I took Floyd to a game with me and I got a call from Charmayne during the game, "Mama, where you at? I see Uncle Floyd on TV right now."

Even as we got older, and far removed from those old days back in Roseland, I always took care of them, just like when we were young. Even though they were all married, if something happened, they would call and tell me, and I would talk to their wives or husbands about it.

"You got them spoiled," they would always tell me. "That's all it is, is you've got them spoiled." I sure do miss the ones who've past on now.

It was around the year 2000 when Sandra got sick. That's when we found out she had ovarian cancer, and it was too far gone to really treat. Around that same time, Gary Floyd also became sick. I pretty much took care of him. I would go get him, and we would go together to the hospital to see her. Just like my mother always told me to do, I helped my sisters and brothers, no matter what. Sandra passed away in

2002.

My brother Willie came with me and we went out to see Floyd in the hospital when his condition got worse. Floyd was really sick, in a hospital bed, but still thinking about me. He would ask me, are you going to the game, Sis?"

"Naw, I need to stay at the hospital with you," I said.

"No you go ahead, and go and get me a program," he said. "Since I can't go, I'll like that. Bring one back for me." He didn't care that much about a program. I knew that he only said that to get me to go to the game so I wouldn't miss it.

When I came back, he was sitting on the couch. He said he wanted to get into the wheelchair and go out with me. He just wanted to get out of the room for a while. I had no idea that's the last time I would see him alive. The next day, he had passed away. That was about two years after Sandra passed. I miss them so much. I think about them every day.

9 PRICELESS DREAM

On January 15, 2017, the Dallas Cowboys hosted the Green Bay Packers in a divisional round playoff game. The intensity level in the stadium was at a fever pitch, and The Cowboys were attempting to make a comeback. After falling behind 21-3 in the first quarter, the Cowboys had cut the deficit to 21-13 at halftime. Shortly after the game resumed for the third quarter, Ms. Price was in her favorite spot directly behind the Cowboys bench when a teenaged boy with neatly cut blonde hair and a much older man approached her.

"Excuse me, are you Ms. Price?" he asked.

"Yeah baby," Ms. Price replied.

"I had my grandfather bring me down here," he explains. "I came down here just so I could speak to you."

"Oh Sugar, that's nice," Ms. Price reaches out and greets him with a warm hug. "Let me guess, are you about fifteen?"

"Yes!" he lights up in excitement following her accurate estimate. "I just love you so much, I told my grandfather 'we have to go down, I don't know when I'll get another chance.' Can I get a picture with you?"

"Of course darling," Ms. Price replies. "We'll

make it look really good.

The boy's grandfather positions his phone and takes a couple of pictures of them. He smiles and nods graciously at Ms. Price, "Thank you Ms. Price."

"You're welcome, you've got a very respectful young man here," she replies. Turning back to the boy she says, "Make sure that you study and obey your parents and your grandfather all of the time, you understand?"

"Yes, ma'am, I will," he answers.

"You can't get anywhere if you don't do that," she says.

In the middle of the biggest Cowboys game of the past few years, a playoff game, with all of the excitement going on in the stadium, and all of the players not more than a few yards away on the sideline, this young fan had completely taken his attention off Dak, Zeke, Dez, Romo and all of the other players who were close enough to pitch a penny at, and was standing in awe of the fact that he finally got a chance to meet Ms. Price.

When I come home, I always turn on my television and I watch the same programs. I always look at the news, spiritual channels, and sports programs. If I see something bad about my Cowboys, like trouble with the law, I don't like it. I don't like to see them do things they have no business doing, but I know they're human and they make mistakes. One day, I picked up my phone and saw a lot of missed calls from people from the Cowboys, even a couple of the players' moms. In my mind, I knew it had to be something pretty bad with everyone calling at the same time. I was wondering what was going on and I finally returned a call to one of the parents.

"Hi, how you doing?" I asked.

"You don't know do you?" she asked. The life kind of went out of me a little bit when she said that. One of our young players, Josh Brent, had been driving under the influence and had a car accident that claimed the life of his teammate, Jerry Brown. It was devastating. I had just taken such a pretty picture with him at one of the ESPN shows, as a matter of fact, with both of them. They were really good friends with each other.

The following week, Josh was suspended, but was allowed on the sideline with his teammates, and the media made a huge deal out of it. It was a terrible thing for them to do that. He was clearly suffering from what he had done. Here's a young man who made a dreadful mistake, but loved Jerry more than any of these people who had something to say about it. He was suffering through the loss of a friend, the guilt of knowing he caused it, and the reality that he had to go on trial and face the possibility of going to prison. Wasn't that enough?

Even though he made a mistake, that didn't mean he didn't deserve to be around the people he loved. They had us on the news together that day. He came up and hugged me and I told him that I was praying for him. The media came over to talk to me after that trying to ask me what our conversation was about.

"I don't have anything to say to you," I told them. What could I say? There was no reason for me to comment on that situation to them. When something like that happens, it's not for me to speak on, so I don't like when they try that with me.

I've had the opportunity to meet so many other players from other teams as well. I met Chris Carter, Corey Dillon, and Rodney Peete: there's a long list of them. I knew Terrell Owens, T.O., long before he came to the Cowboys, when he was still with the 49ers. I went down on the field and went over and took a picture with him. The funny thing is, he signed it later for me when he was playing for The Cowboys but he's in the 49ers uniform on the picture.

I remember when the team first signed Brandon Carr and brought him over from the Kansas City. I know I'm just a woman and a lot of people think we don't really study the players and we just stand around screaming, but I really do study them when they come in. In one of the first games he played, he made an interception that won the game, and afterwards, he came over and took a picture with me. The Associated Press put the picture up. He was at a talk show after the game, and I was there and got a chance to visit with him. He told me that he knew of me before he got to Dallas too.

"Every time I look up in the stands, I see you," he said. "You always have everything laid out so neat with your jewelry and your scarf and everything.

A lot of it has a lot to do with me going to the training camps. That's what separated me from a lot of people because I would not only go to the games, which a lot of people do, but I fly out to the training camp in Oxnard, California. There were two different HBO Hard Knocks segments featuring me: one in '02 and one in around '08. They get more personal with me there. Hard Knocks is a show that HBO does each season where they choose a team to profile and show all of their behind-the-scenes footage at training camp and practices leading up to the season. I've had some memorable moments on there with my Cowboys.

I think a lot of the players gravitate towards me because they see that mother figure that they need to help keep them grounded. The majority of them are from other states, and only a few are from Texas. Most of them don't have that type of figure around them. Jason Witten, our tight end, is another player who really took to me and always showed me the utmost love and respect.

One time, when we were in Houston for a game, Jason Witten's grandparents were there, and they had the area roped off after the game for the fans. Jason came out and found them. He looked over and saw me and brought them over and introduced them to me.

"Stay here with Ms. Price until I come back," he told them.

"I'll take care of them," I told him. They

were very nice people.

One time we were in Atlanta for a game, and I was standing in the lobby just mingling with people, talking and taking pictures.

"Hi," a guy came up to me and spoke.

"Oh my goodness!" I was excited, but a lot of people hanging around me were confused and didn't know who he was. "If you're true blue, you should know who he is," I told them.

It was Jason Witten's brother. He looks just like Jason, so I knew who he was by just looking. He came over and got me while I was standing in the lobby.

"Ms. Price, come over and meet my mother and my brothers," he offered.

He brought me over to meet them and some other friends who were with them. They told me that Jason talks about me. Jason Whitten talks about me? I can't imagine why they would want to talk about me. I don't think of it as having celebrity status or anything. I'm not the one out on the field. I think about it as just having fun and living a dream. There were about four or five of the other wives around, and I was getting ready to go into the game.

Jason's wife asked, "Where do we go to get our passes?" I went over and found a security guard to help them. We stood there and took pictures, and when I was walking away I heard one of them explaining, "That's Ms. Price."

I had the opportunity to meet so many of the

players' moms and other family members. With many of them, I developed friendships that went above and beyond the team, and continued long after their sons were active members of the Cowboys. The best example of that is Sherry Carter-Embree, the mother of Quincy Carter.

Quincy Carter was drafted by The Cowboys in 2001. I was just thrilled for Quincy because it was a great opportunity. For years, the NFL as a whole didn't really give black quarterbacks a chance. Warren Moon, who played down in Houston had to play in Canada for years before he got his chance. There were a few others, including Doug Williams, who was the first to win a Super Bowl with the Redskins, but the progress was slow. It picked up more in the 1990's, and finally here we were: this young man was the quarterback of America's team.

I met Sherry for the first time in Houston. The Houston Texans were a new expansion team, and it was our first time playing against them. We were in the team hotel where the players stay before the games. I always make sure I'm down there to greet the players, and they usually come down and mingle with the fans. I saw Sherry wearing a #17 jersey that said, "Q's Mom." *This is Quincy Carter's mom.* She was wearing some little floppy, denim hat like a teddy bear would wear. I went up to introduce myself, but I couldn't do it without mentioning the hat she was wearing.

"What is going on with that hat darling? Do

you realize that you are the mom of the quarterback of America's team?" I asked her. She didn't take it as an insult, and I think that's why we hit it off. It was just that she was such a humble person and a woman of God. She didn't look at it like she was in some important position. I'll tell you this though: being the quarterback of America's team might not be as important as being The President of the United States, but it is close, ha! From there, we just struck up a really nice conversation and we exchanged phone numbers.

As we got to know each other better, she began to invite me to certain events with her. One year when we were out in California, we were staying in the same hotel, so we just shared a rental car and moved around together the entire time we were out there. We really formed a close bond. We began to do everything together. One time we were hanging out at the hotel by the pool and there were some fans who didn't know who we were.

"Hey, this is Quincy Carter's mom," I was trying to introduce her so they know. "This is the quarterback's mom." But she was trying to introduce me like I was a bigger deal, "this is Ms. Price, The Dallas Cowboys #1 fan, you don't know who she is?"

We had a lot of really great times. She told me that she used to get nervous a lot of times before games, but once she got with me, it helped to calm her down and feel like everything was ok. She was especially nervous for Quincy that first year, because she felt that he was thrust into the position of being the starting quarterback before he was really ready. They had promised him that he would have time to develop, but he showed that he had the talent to start right away, and he was named the starter for game one of his rookie year. That was a big deal. She looked at it like Emmitt Smith was still there and the expectations were high. She feared that it might be too much for him so early. I just tried my best to comfort her and remind her that everything would be ok.

We began to go to more and more events together. She even came to fellowship with me at my church sometimes. Flozelle Adams, our great offensive lineman at the time, was around a lot. Quincy and Sherry were really close to Flozelle's family. One of Quincy's grade school teachers was actually Flozelle's cousin, so he looked out for them a lot when they moved to Dallas and helped them get settled in.

If Flozelle was having an event, Sherry would ask, "Did you invite Ms. Price? Make sure you invite her." I appreciated that she always thought about me. One day we were having a conversation about God and she told me something that was put on her heart.

"Ms. Price, I think this is really your ministry," she said. "To be around these players so you can speak righteousness into their lives. That's what God gave me to tell you," she added. "When those guys don't have their family around them, or if they just need a word of wisdom, you're always there to give that to them. Take that to heart, and know that it's about more than just being the #1 fan. You're more than a #1 fan, because sometimes instead of family, these guys have the wrong people around them."

I remember when Flozelle purchased a large plot of land for a business that he was building and had a ribbon cutting ceremony for it. We all drove out there from Quincy's house, and it was pretty late when we got back there.

"It doesn't make sense for you to try to drive home at this time of night," Sherry said. "Why don't you just spend the night and drive in the morning?" I'm always trying to avoid imposing on people, so I tried to insist that I drive home, but she wouldn't have it. I told her I didn't have any clothes to stay over, and she told me she had a wardrobe there at Quincy's house, and she would give me something to wear. She just kept insisting that I stay, so finally I agreed to. That's the type of heart she has, and she's been a real friend since I met her.

We were down at training camp one year and she had forgotten her ID badge. I think she may have left it at the hotel, and these guys at the gate were giving her trouble. They wouldn't let her in. Imagine that! The mother of the quarterback of America's team, and you're hassling her at the gate to get into a training camp practice? Well, I thought that was just ridiculous. I marched right up to them.

"Look, this is Quincy Carter's mother and I

suggest you let her in! Are you serious?" I said a lot more besides that too. By the time I got finished, we walked right in, ha! She really got a kick out of that. Here I was, the fan, having to get the quarterback's mom into practice. That was pretty hilarious to us.

I was really close to Quincy. I used to meet up and have a few words with him before the games, and I would pray with him. Quincy got better and better as he grew into the position. In his third year, he led the team to a 10-6 record, and into the playoffs for the first time since Troy Aikman was the quarterback.

The next season, during training camp, everything seemed to be going well until one day in early August. I spoke to Sherry that morning. I could tell in her voice her that something had happened, but she wouldn't tell me what.

"You'll see when you get to camp," she told me.

When I got there, the guy at the VIP desk picked up the intercom device and said, "Ms. Price is here."

"Why did you do that?" I asked him.

"Well, they were just kinda concerned—"

"Concerned about what? What are you talking about?" That's when I found out that Quincy had been let go from the team for failing a drug test. Later on, it came out that he had already failed a couple before that. Drugs: there was that word again. I thought back to the day before when I saw some of the security talking to him, and I wondered why they were over there sitting down with him like that.

It really broke my heart. When I saw Sherry, I was actually crying and she wasn't. She was actually consoling me! It was just a sad situation. After Quincy was dismissed from the team, Tony Romo became the quarterback of America's Team. All these years later, Tony is still one of the best quarterbacks in the league. I have no doubt in my mind that Quincy had the talent to do everything that Tony has done in becoming a successful NFL quarterback. It's just another reminder of how the choices that we make have such an impact on our lives.

Another team mom that I became really close friends with was Irma Spears, the mother of Marcus Spears. I met Marcus in 2005 at a rookie signing event. I always love meeting the new rookies because it's like a bunch of new family members coming into the house at once.

"Hey, my baby. Welcome to Dallas," I told Marcus. I have him a big hug and kiss on the cheek and we hit it off from there. I started talking to Marcus and it was like I had known him for his entire life. From that day forward, it stayed that way and that's how I developed a close relationship with his mother Irma. I ended up traveling to some away games with her and she's always been a great friend to me, and remains that way now.

One day, back at the old stadium, I was walking through the stands on the way to my seat, and I saw a woman and her six-year old daughter cheering at the top of their lungs. I just thought the little girl was so adorable.

"Darling, you've got to be the cutest little thing I've ever seen," I told the young girl. "Would you like to go down on the field and meet the players?" I asked. She looked me up and down and then looked over at her mom.

"Hello, I'm Ms. Price," I extended my hand to her mom.

"I'm Cary," she shook my hand, "and this is Ravin," she clenched her daughter's shoulder.

"Hi, Ravin," I said.

"Hello," Ravin replied.

"Can she go down with me?" I asked Cary.

"Yeah, that's fine." She didn't know me from anywhere but for some reason she trusted me with her daughter. I thought maybe she knew who I was, but she told me later she had no idea. She assumed that I must be one of the player's mothers. Down on the field, they got a chance to meet a bunch of players and everyone welcomed us with open arms. T.O., Bobby Carpenter and Zach Thomas were a few of the players who came over to speak to us. I was used to it, but it was great to see them get the opportunity to experience that. Cary took a lot of pictures, so when we got ready to leave, I handed her one of my business cards and told her to e-mail me the pictures. She e-mailed me the pictures and I thanked her.

We spoke from time to time and she told me she lived in Oklahoma and was a school teacher in both junior high and high school. As training camp approached for the next season, I thought about them and sent Cary an e-mail and asked, "Would you like to attend training camp with me?" She was surprised by the offer. She checked with her husband and told me that it would be ok. I told her to get a ticket to San Antonio and I would meet her at the airport and pick her up, which I did. I picked her up in my Cadillac and we rode up to training camp. Several of the players like Sam Hurd and Keith Brooking were coming up to the car to speak and I was blasting "My Heroes Have Always Been Cowboys," by Willie Nelson.

At the hotel, we got off the elevator and ran into Jerry Jones' grandchildren. I introduced Ravin to them and they hit it off. We had a great time. That was about twelve years ago, and since then, we've only missed one training camp together. I bring her with me on the other side of the rope, as David Wells had done for me so many times years before, and when we're together she never lets me pay for a meal. Ravin has been attending the Cowboys' cheerleader camps for years, and now at age 17, she'll finally be old enough to try out to be a Dallas Cowboys cheerleader next year. We dream of seeing her run out onto that field with the rest of those beautiful young ladies at every home game. That would be great. Sometimes I'm just drawn to people and God puts it on my heart to know that they are truly good people. I have so many stories like this of meeting the nicest people and striking up lifelong friendships because of my Dallas Cowboys family.

I remember when I first met Lawrence Vickers, who played fullback for us. He's a very courteous person. He said he knew who I was before he got to the Cowboys. He told me the players used to have a contest in the locker room to see who could sound the most like me, ha! He said Tony Romo, and maybe two or three others did a really good Ms. Price impersonation. Imagine that!

I remember one time when we were in the middle of that playoff run with Quincy, I was just standing there watching the game. I was broken up over that game because we were losing and it was still up in the air whether or not we would make the playoffs. I looked down and I saw this figure coming towards me and then I recognized him. "There's Emmitt," I said, "I wonder where he's going."

"I'm coming to see you," he said.

"Oh my God!" I hugged him. He sat and spoke with me awhile. I was really torn up behind that game, so I felt a little bit better then.

When Dave Campo was our head coach, one day he told me, "the players really love you." I was speechless.

He said, "They really do speak about you and appreciate you."

"I've never thought of it that way," I replied.

I was shocked, but as I got a chance to be around more, I wasn't as surprised. I never stopped loving it less though. Someone who really, really loved me was Greg Ellis, our big defensive end from that era. I don't know if I looked like someone he knew or what. That's what it seemed like because he just took to me immediately, like I was a long, lost relative.

I think the biggest surprise was during one of our losing seasons, we had lost three games in a row, and the next game was in New York. I made reservations for the New York game and I knew they had no idea I would be there. When the Cowboys team bus pulled in, I was standing on the corner. I think one of the first players' faces I saw was Tony. They all started waving at me on the bus. I went over when they got off and they were happy to see me. Dez Bryant came up and hugged me.

"When did you get here?" Miles Austin asked.

"I've been here just waiting on y'all," I told him.

It's the personal moments with the players that really stir something inside of me. When you get right down to it, they're just people. They feel all of the same emotions we do. Watching them play the game on the field, or on TV can make them seem larger than life. I love those little interactions with them that remind me that they're just like all the rest of us.

Sean Lee has been one of the most consistent and important players that we've had on our team for several years. I remember when he first arrived as a rookie. He came to our team in 2010. That was the same year Jason Garrett became the coach. In fact, he was just the interim coach at the time. Coach Wade Phillips had gotten replaced in the middle of the season after the team got off to a bad start. Jason wasn't even guaranteed to keep the job yet. He was in the process of trying to earn it.

Keith Brooking was starting at linebacker, and Sean Lee was his backup. Brooking was one of the main leaders on the team that year, and was actually having a really good season. Sean hadn't been playing much. He was just getting his feet wet, and learning the ropes of the NFL.

During the annual Thanksgiving Day game, Brooking got hurt, and Sean had to take over. This was against the New Orleans Saints and we lost a really close game by three points. The game the following week was against the Indianapolis Colts on their home field. Of course, at this time, Peyton Manning was still the quarterback of the Colts and he's one of the best ever. Brooking wasn't better yet, and Sean had to start in his place. Sean was really nervous. He'll tell you to this day. His first time starting and carrying that responsibility and he had to go toe-to-toe with Manning.

I had a chance to see him the day before the game at the team hotel. He had been on my heart because I knew how he must be feeling in that situation. He had big shoes to fill. Brooking was one of the main guys that really got everybody going and ready to play. I went over to him and hugged him.

"How you doing darling?"

"I'm fine Ms. Price, how about you?"

"I'm great. Are you nervous?" I asked.

"A little bit," he smiled.

"Well, I just want you to know that you've been in my prayers. I see great things for you. You are going to go out there and play great tomorrow. You'll see. You're going to be the story. We're going to be talking about you and what you did." It was the truth. I had been thinking about him like I would anybody else I cared about who was about to go through a life changing experience.

"I hope you're right," he replied.

"Ms. Price is right," I told him. "Watch what I tell you."

That next day, it was a really close game, and we were hanging onto the lead, 20-14, towards the end of the third quarter. Peyton Manning threw the ball towards one of his receivers, and Sean was right there to intercept it. He just read his eyes and was right there to make the play. He took the interception and ran it all the way back for a touchdown. Imagine that: not only an interception, but a touchdown in his very first game starting. He wasn't finished though.

The game pretty much swung back and forth after that and we ended up with the score tied, and we had to go to overtime. In overtime, Manning had a pass tipped and Sean was right there in position to make the play again: another interception. He ran it back far enough to put us in field goal range. We ended up kicking the field goal and winning by three points. Sean was the hero that game with a touchdown and two interceptions, with the second one clinching the game.

When I saw him after the game, he gave me a big hug and said, "You called it." I was so happy for him. He never looked back, and from that season on, he's been our starting linebacker and one of the best players on our defense.

My voice is very distinguishable and that helps because the players can hear me over a lot of other people. More than anything, I just want to see them win a championship again so badly. I know they will. I just know we will. I think I'll write Stephen, Jerry's son, a letter with some suggestions about what we can do to adjust. Stephen is really nice. I think he probably has more of his mother Gene's personality. All of them are such nice people. They really turned this city around. No one really knows how much they love their fans. They judge them from the outside, but I've been blessed to really just sit and talk and go out to Valley Ranch and stand around and see Jerry walk up saying, "Hey Girl!"

Stephen has beautiful children also. I've seen them grow up. They run up to me and give me hugs after the game, and they're so sweet. I know that one day, these will be the leaders of The Cowboys. I just pray that before Jerry gets too old and retires, he gets a chance to win a couple more championships. I really want to see that for him. I've seen Roosevelt, his security man, have to almost pull him away while he's signing autographs to the point where his hand is just shaking. That's when they're traveling, not just in Dallas. That's the side of Jerry that people don't hear about. He loves the people. It's just been a blessing that I've been able to do a few things with them.

One time Judy said, "Carolyn, I look at you as Cinderella."

"What do you mean?" I asked.

"I see it like the people who treated you badly and did things to try to keep you down were the stepsisters, but then Cinderella is the one that married the prince. All of this fun you're having, the notoriety with the Cowboys and all of this, that's like your prince. It's like you were down all that time and all of a sudden all of this came to you." I thought that was a lovely way to put it.

Dallas has some true blue fans all over, but we could get a little more vocal sometimes to help our team out more. We all love our team, but we're not known to be one of those fan bases that just drown everything out with noise, and make it hard for the other team to concentrate. I guess maybe we're a little too cool sometimes. One time, Troy Aikman was on the radio and he said "if the fans get more like Ms. Price, other teams won't want to come into the stadium to play." I agree Troy, ha!

As much as people have things to say about

the Cowboys, so many want to be like them. Now look around at how many teams have the star. The Titans have it now. When Houston came back in existence, they used it. They can't use a solid star, but they all have a variation of it. New England went from just a patriot with his hand on the football, to that thing with a star on his helmet. They all want to have that image like The Cowboys. I don't have a problem with it. I like being somebody that others want to look like.

If you look nice, I may say, "Hey, where did you get those shoes?" Maybe I'll get a pair like it. I don't want to look like a bum. These other teams don't either, so that's a good thing. You don't think Jerry's a dummy do you? He's the one that went with Nike first and now everybody's wearing it. Even your grandmother has on a Nike cap.

A lot of the players stay close to the team and it really is like a family. I saw Larry Allen a lot recently. I'm so happy that Nate Newton made it into the Hall of Fame. Robert Newhouse had a stroke a while back but he's better now. I called his daughter one day and I surprised her. He has a set of twins. They're such sweet girls.

One time, one of the reporters from the local ESPN station was at the hotel eating and I ran into him.

"How you doing Ms. Price? He asked.
"I'm fine," I told him.
"You know if you were cheering for

Cincinnati, people wouldn't have any idea who you were," he reasoned. "They would think you were some lunatic," he laughed.

He went on to the other teams, like Detroit and Tampa Bay, "can you imagine sitting there with a ship on the side of your head or some curly, little lion on your head?" It was so funny the way he explained it.

"Shut up talking to me!" By this point I was laughing really hard because it was really hilarious thinking about it. Imagine me jumping up and down with a lion in my hand saying, "Go Detroit!" People would think, "What a lulu bird."

A lot of times, I affect people in ways that I could never even imagine. People come up to me later and tell me how I affected them in a certain way and it really warms my heart. There was a young lady that was on my job: she's not there anymore.

She called me a little while back, and nobody knows she did, but she said, "Ms. Price, I just wish I had listened to you more and I thank you for helping me." At one point, she was on her way to get an abortion and I stopped her. Now, she has a little girl and a little boy.

I'm not a hard person. I just communicate with people. When I call them, they're in my office in less than ten seconds, and when I hit the phone and ring that bell, they answer my question. I'm not mean. I fully believe that you reap what you sow, so I treat people like I want to be treated, and I expect the same. I have to call a spade a spade.

As many unexpected tragedies as we have endured in the family, nothing could prepare me for a call that I received from my sister one day in 2011. Phyllis called me and said, "Carolyn, it's on the news that Rasool just drowned his two little boys." Rasool was my brother Buck's son.

"Are you kidding me?" I was floored. I was at work, and I had to leave immediately. I had a lot of emotions at one time. I had just saw them at a wedding recently, and then this happened.

Buck had to see it from the hospital room because he had gone in the hospital the day before it happened. They were living with him at the time. We tried to go out to the hospital to tell him before he saw it on the news, but he had already seen it. Apparently, Rasool was reacting to some type of drugs, someone said something about embalming fluid, I don't know. But there's that word again: drugs.

I have no doubt that was the case, because how else could somebody ever do something that horrible? I can only imagine it was drugs because there was never anything that he showed to make anyone think that he was capable of that. We're no match for these drugs. He was very nice, but he didn't seem to have found his purpose. When I'd see him, I'd get on him about working, going to school and doing something with his life. Idle hands are the devil's workshop.

Buck and his wife separated when Rasool was young. They had a daughter also. They both were struggling with their own drug problems. I spent as much time helping out as I could. Rasool's grandmother, his mother's mother, helped out as much as she could with them also, and really did a lot for them. Through their graduations and proms, I stood there with them as much as I could, but the circumstances around them meant that those kids were left on their own a lot. They spent a lot of time fending for themselves and making a way to survive. When I would find out they were in a certain neighborhood, I would always tell someone I knew around there to look out for them and let me know if they were doing something that they had no business doing. One time, I went by and spoke with one of their neighbors.

"I'm going to give you my number," I told her. "Please keep an eye on them and if something happens, or if there's a need, call me."

"I will sure do that," she told me. She was really nice. It wasn't more than a week later when she called.

"Remember you told me that if something happened over here to call you and let you know?"

"Yes, I remember," I braced for the bad news.

"What happened?"

"Their mom just got shot," she said. She was critically injured, but she recovered. It wasn't the last call I got. There was a lot going on around them, but this situation with Rasool was above and beyond anything imaginable.

On the day of the incident, Rasool's sons were walking to school with their mom when he pulled up in a car. The older son, Naim, was five years old. It was his first day of kindergarten. He was named after Rasool. Rasool is actually his middle name. He used a brick to force all three of them to get into the car and drove off. While the car was stopped at the intersection, the children's' mother was able to escape from the car and flag down a constable. She must have thought the constable would chase Rasool and stop him, but he didn't. He called police offers instead.

In Dallas, constables carry a gun and badge like police officers but their main job is to issue warrants and serve legal papers. She later called 911 when she found the bodies of the boys. When they found Rasool, he confessed. He gave them the confession on video. Later on, during the trial, they played his taped confession back in front of him. He described in detail the act of drowning his two sons.

It was a heart-wrenching moment for everyone in the courtroom, including Rasool. He cried so loudly while the confession was playing that people heard him outside in the hallway. Two years after the fact, with a sober mind, it must have seemed like he was listening to someone else describe the events of that dreadful day. Whatever triggered the problem in the first place, I do not believe you can be in your right mind and commit a crime like that. To take the life of your own children can only be the effect of real mental illness.

Arguing on behalf of Rasool's life, his lawyer blamed his mother and claimed that he grew up around violence and sexual abuse. He told the court that this should be enough reason to spare him from the death penalty, and give him a life sentence. The jury disagreed. They sentenced him to death. He apologized to everyone. He said that the reason he did it was because he just wanted to be a father and felt like that was being taken away from him. He and the children's mother were no longer together and she had moved on and began dating someone else.

I had to be there for my brother. These were his grandchildren. How do you make sense out of a situation like that? Those are your babies. I asked him to come and live with me but he wouldn't. I guess that's just me still trying to take care of everyone. It's what I know how to do. My sister calls me sometimes worried about him and vice versa. He calls me when it gets to him sometimes and he gets really upset about it.

People who deal with me trust me and what I say because they know I mean it. People will ask me to do things, and if I can, I usually will, because I just like to help people. One time, a guy I met, who's a college professor in New York, wanted to get a letter to one of the Cowboys' players. He sent it to me because he figured that I could get it to them. I did it for him. I get called on for favors like that a lot. It might seem odd to a lot of other people but it's normal to me.

As far as dealing with the players, I look at it like any other person, or even an animal for that matter: if you pet him, he'll wiggle his tail, if you scold him, he might snap at you. People can tell when people are being mean. I won't sit here and say that every player that I've dealt with was really nice, but there's also no instance that would make me say, "Let me sit here and tell you how mean this Dallas Cowboy was." I would be lying. For some, they might not have done anything except wave, but they would at least do that. With others, we may speak after every game, pray together, or do appearances together at events. I can tell you this though: I've met most of them, each and every year, in each and every decade of the team's existence.

Dallas has always been involved with so many teams that were considered rivals that it ended up enhancing the team's identity even more. Even if we lost the game, we were always involved in these tight games that were considered classic and made history. To be honest, me personally, I've never cared about who we played. I just always wanted to win. I'm not interested in who's on your team. I don't care you your quarterback is. I don't care who your receivers are. I don't care. It never made me any difference.

I've always gotten favorable coverage in the

media. They are really drawn to me. Not just the local stations either. Channel 8 in Oxnard, California has covered me several times and did a really nice feature on me when we were out there for training camp.

When Cowboys Stadium opened in 2009, the network Tru TV, did a special profile on their show NFL Full Contact. Over 100,000 people were present for the event. They focused on all of the different aspects of the opening of the stadium, from the people behind the scenes running the technical parts of the show, the players, the coaches, and then all of a sudden the camera cut to... Ms. Price, the Dallas Cowboys #1 Fan.

It was a pretty funny segment. I got a lot of response from that one. The first shot shows me standing in my front yard. "I didn't sleep hardly last night, and every time you turn on the television, there they are on ESPN, talking about the Dallas Cowboys!" I couldn't contain the excitement. I had seen the transition of going from playing at the old Cotton Bowl stadium to Texas Stadium in 1971. This was a completely different ball game.

Cowboys Stadium, which has since been renamed AT&T Stadium, was the stadium of all stadiums: especially when it first opened. It has over 80,000 seats but can hold over 100,000 people with the standing room. The high definition video screen stretches from 20-yard line to 20-yard line and was probably the most talked about part of the stadium.

When they played the NBA All-Star game there, the screen was actually bigger than the basketball court!

Then, they showed me inside of the house getting dressed, and putting on all of my accessories. I had on my #24 Marion Barber jersey that day. Then, they cut to a bunch of shots from a lot of different games when I was cheering on the sidelines. The cameras find me all the time.

"Tony Romo!... Throw it Tony!...Let's go!...You get your popcorn ready!...This is America's Team!" I'm always in the spirit when I'm on the sideline. I can always be heard over everyone around me and that's what always made me stand out.

On another part of the stadium opening segment, I was trying to get my tickets and they were not allowing me to pull into the parking lot. I had to leave my Cadillac where it was, directly in front of the stadium, and walk to get some help. My beautiful car, with my star on the side, was parked right in front of the stadium on national TV for everyone to see. They told me I had to move. When I told them I was parking there temporarily while I got my tickets, they asked who I was with.

"I'm not with anybody," I told them. "I'm a friend of Jerry Jones." There was a countdown until they opened the roof and doors to the stadium, like New Year's Eve.

"5, 4, 3, 2, 1..." and the massive roof on top of the stadium slid back to reveal the bright, sunny sky.

The festive mood lasted throughout the game and we had a great time cheering for our team. The game was a tight one and we were holding on to a one point lead, 31-30, when the New York Giants drove down field and got in position to take the lead. All we could do was watch, pray and hope that their kicker missed a kick at the end that would let us hold the lead. He didn't. All I could do is drop my head into my hands as the ball went through the goal posts with no time left and we lost the first game in the new stadium 33-31.

I stood down in the tunnel under the stadium where the players leave. I always want to see them afterwards, win or lose, but when we lose, I always want to say a few words to them when I can.

"Bye Tony," I said to Tony Romo as he got on the back of a golf court to exit the stadium.

"See you later, you hear? I love you," I told him as I hugged him.

"Preciate it," he replied hugging me back. He was really down, and I know he takes a lot of the weight on his shoulders because he's the quarterback. I know the last thing he could have imagined was losing the first game in the new stadium, to the Giants of all teams. He was clearly upset. So many of the players were. I saw Marcus Spears and went up to Marcus to console him.

"You're going to enjoy a lot of victories in this place," I told him. "This is just one. Let it go, and get ready for next Sunday." He looked up and managed to smile.

"You actually sounded like a coach when you said that," he replied. I got a good laugh out of that one. As the players walked through the tunnel towards the locker room I screamed, "24-hour rule! 24-hour rule!" It was just my little reminder of what the coaches always tell them. You have to let the game go and get to the next one whether it's after a win or a loss. You can't get too high or too low about one game during a long season.

Then just as most of the players had gone, and I had spoken to as many as I could, a special guest came walking through. Is that LeBron James? It sure was LeBron James.

"Oh my God, I was wanting to see you!" I fidgeted around looking for my camera. I couldn't believe it was him. I don't get what they call star struck over seeing many people, but seeing LeBron there caught me off guard though. I got my camera and gave it to one of the guys standing around to take a picture for me. He put his arm around me and posed for the camera. He was huge standing over me. The guy snapped the camera.

"Now turn it around and take another one," I directed.

"Yeah, turn it the long way," LeBron added.

"So they can see how sexy we are," I said.

"Uh-huh," he replied.

"Remember that girl that was heckling you at that game?" I asked.

"Uh huh, what's wrong with her?" he asked jokingly. He was so down to earth and polite. When he got ready to walk off I hugged him probably tighter than he expected, ha! I kissed him on the cheek and he gave me one in return.

"Love you baby," he said.

"Bye baby," I said as he walked off. "Yeah!" That was a good way to temporarily lift my spirits and take my mind off the loss. To think, if he wasn't such a big Cowboys fan, I probably never would have met him. The biggest superstar in the NBA, who was born, raised and playing in Ohio, is a true blue Cowboys fan. That should tell you something about us.

Next, they showed a clip from training camp when the players were running by and I got Marc Colombo's attention. "Colombo! Come here baby," I motioned for him to come over. "Give Mama a hug," I stretched my arms out to him. He came over and hugged me.

"How you doing?" he asked. I hugged him tightly.

Then they cut to a shot of our head coach at the time, Wade Phillips telling the team to break it down on Ms. Price. When the teams break it down, they all chant a word that means something significant to the team.

"1, 2, 3...TEAMWORK," or "1, 2, 3...DEFENSE!" It's usually something of that nature. This time was different.

"Ms. Price on three, here we go," Coach Phillips said, extending his hand in the air. All of the players laughed at the instruction before gathering around in a huddle.

"1, 2, 3," Coach Phillips said.

"MS. PRICE!" the team called out all at once. I didn't see it when they actually did it. Coach Phillips came over and spoke to me and told me they had done it. When he told me, I let out the biggest laugh. I thought it was great. I saw it later on TV and it just warmed my heart. The guys have fun with me and get a kick out of me. That's why I love training camp so much. It allows me to really get up close and personal with the players. I give all of them my special form of motivation. It's not just the popular players. All of them are my Cowboys.

"What's going on Clint Stoerner!" I yelled one practice at our former backup quarterback.

"Not a thing," he chuckled as he walked through a drill where they stepped over a group of small hurdles.

"Let's get it going! Let's get it going, Stoerner!" I hollered.

"You got it going," he shot back.

"You got it going!" I replied. They know that if they are on the side of the field near me, they are going to hear me all day. Sometimes I would manage to slide a lot closer to the field than where I was supposed to be. It's not that it was necessarily on purpose, but when I'm wrapped up in what my boys are doing I just tend to drift closer and closer to the action.

"Ma'am, blue passes have to stay back over there," a man on the sideline told me. "You're too close to where the players are. Somebody will come off and hit you."

"I ain't gon do nothing but love it," I told him. One day after practice, I saw George Teague, our former safety, and approached him.

"George, I'm getting ready to hug that neck," I warned him.

"I just got done doing all this running," he said.

"You think Ms. Price care?" I asked.

"No," he reached out and tried to hug me from a distance so he wouldn't get sweat on me as I hugged his neck.

"You look like you're in pretty good shape like you lost some weight," I said.

"202 today," George replied.

"What are you going to do for me this year?" I asked.

"I'll do what I always do."

"Are you going to bring it to the house for me?"

"Always," he answered.

Sam Hurd, who used to play wide receiver for us, said I gave him a wet, nasty kiss.

"She gave me the nastiest, wet kiss ever on my cheek," he said. "It was like a grandma kiss completely. She was like 'hey baby!" He imitated my voice and everything, ha! I sure did darling. Sam was another player who ended up having some problems with drugs, and as always, I hated to hear it. It hurt me to my heart. It's just such a recurring theme in life: these drugs destroy people's lives. He is such a sweet, mannerable young fellow.

The coaches get the same treatment. They are not exempt at all.

"Dave Campo!" I yelled one time as our former coach came walking onto the practice field.

"Ms. Price, how are you?" he replied.

"What's going on baby!" I called to him.

"How you doing?" he asked.

"Come give me my lucky hug," I said.

"Yes ma'am, I'm coming right there," he replied as he walked over. He knew the routine too.

They're all my boys.

When T.O. got to Dallas, there was a lot of attention around him. During his career with two other teams, he had always proved to be one of the best players in the league. He also had a reputation for getting into it with different people but that didn't matter to me any. I judge people by how they treat me and what I see with my own eyes and hear with my own ears. I met him long before he even came to the Cowboys and he treated me nicely. He played for us from 2006-2008.

He told Tony Romo that I was his alarm clock while they were on the sideline at practice.

Then Tony Romo started imitating me calling out Terrell's name. How many people can say they've experienced that? It's nothing but God.

There was one stretch where people were kind of down on T.O., and he had some type of argument with the wide receivers coach. He really needed to have a big game to snap him out of it. He bounced back in a game against the Houston Texans. In the first half, it was a slow game, and we barely had the lead. T.O. had a huge second half and scored three touchdowns.

After the game, Fox television was interviewing me for a segment called "Fan on the Street," and we were talking about T.O.

"I'm just glad T.O. was able to show what he really can do," I told the reporter. "I was really praying for that and it really happened. I'm excited about that. We had a wonderful game." Right in the middle of our conversation, T.O. came driving towards us to exit the parking lot.

"Here comes Mr. T.O. now," I pointed to a burnt orange Range Rover trying to get through the remaining crowd and the media gathered around. I knew he didn't want to talk to the media, but I'm not the media.

"He'll talk to me," I told them as I walked towards him. I walked right up to the driver's side window and motioned for him to let the window down.

"Mama prayed for you," I said as he rolled

the window down. "Listen, I'm serious. Ms. Price love you," I continued as T.O. nodded.

"I am there for you and I know that you can do good. Keep focused and listen to what Mama tell you, ok?" T.O. nodded and smiled.

"When the media talks, just say, 'ok'," I told him, which made him laugh. "Say Ms. Price told me not to say nothing. But keep your popcorn ready!" That was a reference to his favorite catchphrase, "get your popcorn ready," meaning he was about to put on a show.

"T.O., I love you baby, bye bye," I told him as he pulled off. I couldn't believe how some of the fans had turned on him when they thought he wasn't doing as well as they expected. What kind of fan is that? These are our players, and I don't believe in that. I wanted to lift him up, and I was so happy for him that he had such a great game and got back on track.

Just as I've become closer with certain players, parents and people in the organization than others, the same goes for people in the media. When you come across enough good people on a regular basis, you're bound to forge special bonds with some. I met Yulonda Hadnot during training camp in 2015 on the very first day of camp. She's a television reporter that covers the Cowboys for KTEV-TV in Texarkana. She was walking with her producer, just looking around taking everything in, and she looked like she was really amazed at what she was seeing.

She was there as a reporter, but I can spot a true fan when I see one. I was really proud to see a young, African-American woman out there covering our team. I thought she looked very pretty and thought I'd introduce myself.

"Hey! Hey!" I yelled at her to get her attention over all of the other surrounding noise. I finally had to grab her because I don't think she knew I was talking to her.

"You are so beautiful," I told her.

"Thank you," she had a really kind demeanor as she spoke. She was surprised and I could tell that she didn't understand why I had singled her out, but the Lord speaks to me about people.

"I see great things over your life," I told her. "I see great things in your future." I didn't say that just to say it. I don't say anything just to say it. If I say it, I mean it. From that quick introduction, we hit it off and built a relationship, just as I've done with so many other good people in my life. She told me later that she didn't have any idea who I was when I first introduced myself to her and when she asked her producer who I was, he simply told her, "Google Dallas Cowboys #1 Fan and tell me what you see."

She had several other interviews planned regarding a bunch of different storylines around the team, but after she met me and saw who I was, she dropped all of those plans and I became her very first interview at training camp.

During the interview, we had a great time,

and it was more like a conversation with a friend than an interview. I revealed a lot of details about my background and how I ultimately became a Cowboys fan in the first place. We forged a bond based on the fact that we were both women who loved the Cowboys. Throughout the remainder of training camp, we'd see each other, exchange pleasantries, and have conversations about everything that was going on regarding the upcoming season.

On the last day of camp, she approached me, and I told her, "Darling, give me your contact information so we can keep in touch." We exchanged numbers, and we stayed in touch throughout the rest of the summer. Once the season started, she would come over to my area during games just to talk about the game, or take a picture, or just to speak. I would always give her encouraging words to keep her going, because we never know what's going on in a person's life.

Everything can seem great on the surface, but we can all use added encouragement from time to time. I always remind her that she is beautiful, and that she's talented. I visualize her on the sidelines one day for a major network covering our Cowboys just like Pam Oliver does now. I'll be standing right there smiling like a proud mom.

As much as people like to talk trash about sports, for the most part, everyone has always respected my space when it came to the Cowboys. They would always say, "Don't call her right now,

Dallas is playing." If we were getting beat in a real serious game, they would all come around like somebody was sick or something, ha! Then, I would get calls.

"Carolyn, are you alright?" they would ask.

"Yes, I'm alright," I would always reply, whether I was or not. Everyone is always happy when they see me on TV.

On most Sundays, I'm at church faithfully. I am pretty much always there, except for when the time of the game doesn't allow me to be. My pastor knows and respects what I have to do with my Cowboys. I give him a schedule as soon as they come out for the season, so he'll know when to expect me and when not to. My pastor is on my Facebook, so I can't fool him, I have to do right. On the days when I can't make it to church, I'll always catch a service on TV while I'm getting ready for the game. Anybody that's got something to say about Jesus, and I feel in my heart that they are talking from the word, I'll give them a listen.

I teach my kids, be careful what you do, because life is unpredictable, and you never know what it will bring you. You don't know why things happen.

I used to wonder sometimes, "What can I do to do a better job of avoiding things?" As if it's something could actually be controlled. No matter what has happened to me, I've never turned from Jesus. At times, he was my only hope. I always kept going to church and taking my kids to church. I always wanted everyone to be grounded. Also, I always cook and eat some good food, ha! That helps too.

In August of 2016, I received several messages from my ex-husband, Willie Price, members of his family and some of his friends and everyone was telling me that he wanted to see me. I went by to visit him and one day the lady who really gave me a lot of trouble during out marriage was coming out the door as was going in.

"Oh, you're going to get my husband?" she asked. I guess she called herself trying to make a joke.

"No darling, you won," I told her. I went in and he was clearly very sick and I couldn't tell how much longer he would be around. He spoke to me in a very soft voice.

"I saw you on television," he said.

"You did?" I asked. "You must've recognized my voice."

"No, your face," he said. "You still look the same.

"Thank you," I replied.

"I just want to let you know that I'm so sorry for everything I've taken you through," he said.

"Willie, it's not good to pour water on a drowning man," I replied. "God is a healer, and I do understand. I'm not a perfect person and I forgive you."

"Everything you went through with the kids

and all the problems you had, I added to them," he replied.

"It's no problem. Sometimes things happen. One thing about it, yeah, you made a choice, but they knew you were married, and people know what they're doing when they're doing these type of things.

He asked me about Charmayne, Dee, Chloe and how everyone else was doing and I told him they were fine.

"Charde is getting ready to go to college," I told him about our great granddaughter.

"I sure want to help," he said.

"Whatever you want to do is alright with me," I assured him.

He laid there and tears began to roll down his face. It's not every day when that happens and you stand over the bed and see someone in that position who's been unfaithful, and unkind to you. One thing I will always say about him though is that he was a great provider and he took great care of me of my children. His granddaughter Chloe truly adored him. Kids don't know how to hate: they have to be taught to hate. I thank God that he had that opportunity to repent to me and I had the opportunity to repent to him. It was a really blessed moment for me because everybody doesn't get that opportunity. That's why we have to be so careful how we live and I'm so grateful that we got to do that. I thank God for that. A couple of months later, in October, he passed. That was the same month that we had gotten married.

There have been so many things that have happened to me over the course of my life. For a while it just seemed like it was all a big dream. It seemed more like a nightmare when so many negative things were happening back to back. It didn't feel like that could possibly be reality. It actually got to the point where the reality was harder to believe than something that was made up.

Between the deaths of my mom and dad, my oldest sister's murder, the murder of her two children, and the other deaths in the family, I just kept going. It was all I knew to do. I guess it's kind of like when a boxer gets knocked down, and you can tell that they are not back in their right mind yet, but they just get up and keep swinging off instinct. That's how I was. Time and time again, I went to Jesus and asked him to give me strength, and he did. He did it over and over again. I know he's awesome because when I go to bed I sleep so well. How else could I sleep peacefully with so much on my heart? He speaks to me.

I can be just sitting here and he may say, "You didn't pay your water bill," and I'll jump up and pay it. He talks to me all the time. I always tell the Lord that I want to live to be 102 years old, go to sleep and go to Heaven. That's what I always tell Him.

Sometimes, I'll start to say, "Why did you…" and I'll catch myself. "I don't wanna question you," I tell him. Whenever I get really lonely, it seems like the scriptures that relate to that will come to me, or

I'll turn on the TV and the preacher will be preaching about Job or a subject that I need to hear and that will comfort me. This is not a coincidence.

I look at some of my friends, and I'm just amazed that some of their parents are still living. Wow, they got the chance to enjoy their parents all this time. I didn't get that opportunity, but I never wavered in my belief that God's got something for me. There's a reason for all of this. Like I tell my children, "If you do what's right, you don't have to worry about where you stand in life. All you have to do is do what's right." I'm not uncomfortable being alone because I told the Lord that I would rather be alone if I'm not comfortable with someone treating me the right way. I would rather just stay by myself. He blessed me to help my family, and that's good enough for me.

That's where my Cowboys come in. They have been the most consistent part of my life since I lost my parents. I've watched the team grow up as I've grown up. I've watched so many Cowboys come and go, and they were always there for me when I needed them. I always know where they are going to be on Sunday, and I'm always going to be right there with them for the rest of my life.

I am extremely proud of my boys, and I made this same statement to several reporters who asked. When Tony was injured before this past season even began, nobody thought we would go through and come out with a 13-3 record, a first-round bye and home field advantage. Nobody thought that. How could I not be proud? I'm very grateful.

As I went out of that stadium after the last game, that feeling was something that I couldn't hold back just knowing that they did an excellent job. Seeing a player like Jason Witten become the elder statesman who's been through all the battles, and players like Sean Lee and Dez Bryant become the new veterans, and seeing the young players like Dak Prescott, Ezekiel Elliott and Cole Beasley take off is a wonderful feeling. My main thing is that now I know what I have to look forward to. I know the team is in good hands.

All they have to do is keep their heads screwed on right and make sure that they stay focused, and pick up the pattern that Ms. Price has lived by for years: God, family and The Cowboys. I can guarantee you, coming up without parents and the things I've been through, it works. I guarantee you that. I works. It ain't always easy, but it works.

Life is something marvelous to witness, and if I had to live it over, the only thing I would do differently is I wouldn't put so much trust into so many people, and now that I know just how much God is really in control, I would be more careful what I complained about and I would trust him even more.

ABOUT THE AUTHOR

Anwar Jamison is the Lead Faculty of the Digital Media Program at Arkansas State University-Midsouth. He is the writer and director of two feature films: *Funeral Arrangements* and *5 Steps to a Conversation* and a sports columnist for 49erswebzone. He is also an accomplished hip-hop artist and producer who has released several projects under the artist name 2Dash.

A native of Racine, WI, he currently resides in Memphis, TN.

Lightning Source UK Ltd.
Milton Keynes UK
UKHW02f0912021217
313718UK00007BA/227/P

9 780692 842522